BEAT THE IQ CHALLENGE

TEST ◇ YOUR INTELLIGENCE

BEAT THE IQ CHALLENGE

PHILIP J. CARTER &
KEN A. RUSSELL

JOINT EDITORS OF THE MENSA UK PUZZLE GROUP JOURNAL

WARD LOCK

A WARD LOCK BOOK

First published in the UK
1993 by Ward Lock
A Cassell imprint
Villiers House
41/47 Strand
London
WC2N 5JE

Reprinted 1994

Distributed in the United States by Sterling Publishing Co., Inc.
387 Park Avenue South, New York, NY 10016-8810

Distributed in Australia by Capricorn Link (Australia) Pty Ltd
P.O. Box 665, Lane Cove, NSW 2066

British Library Cataloguing-in-Publication Data
A catalogue record for this book is available from the British Library

ISBN 0 7063 7128 3

Design and typesetting by Malca Schotten, illustrations by Ruth Rudd

Printed and bound in Great Britain by Cox & Wyman Ltd, Reading

CONTENTS

ACKNOWLEDGEMENTS

We wish to thank the British Mensa Committee and the Mensa Executive Director, Harold Gale, for their continued support for all our projects. Special thanks are due to members of Enigmasig for their support, interest, inspiration and lively correspondence. A huge amount of thanks goes to our wives, both named Barbara, for their enthusiasm, optimism and invaluable assistance with checking puzzles and preparing the typescript; without their support this book would not have been possible.

Publishers note : All references to Mensa are to British Mensa Ltd.

ABOUT THE AUTHORS

Philip Carter is an engineering estimator and also a Yorkshire JP. He is Editor of *Enigmasig*, the Mensa Special Interest Puzzle Group newsletter.

Ken Russell is a London surveyor and is also Puzzle Editor of *Mensa*, the monthly publication of British Mensa Ltd.

INTRODUCTION

It is with great pleasure that we present the fourth of the IQ Challenge books, which takes the number of puzzles in the series to over 500. Our association as compilers began in 1986 through our membership of Mensa, the high-IQ society, and our involvement with Enigmasig, a special-interest group within Mensa dedicated to the setting and solving of puzzles.

Mensa has many special-interest groups with such diverse interests as astrology, badminton, cats, Dr Who, ecology, films, genealogy, humour, investment, Judaism, literature, Monty Python, photography, quizzes, rambling, Sherlock Holmes, travel and wealth acquisition.

Founded in 1946, Mensa is a society the sole qualification for membership of which is to have attained a score in any supervised test of general intelligence that puts the applicant in the top 2 per cent of the general population. On the Cattell Intelligence Scale this represents an IQ score of 148. The name Mensa is derived from the Latin word for 'table'; and Mensa is a round-table society, which aims to include intelligent people of every opinion and calling. Within the society all members are of equal standing, and no one member or group of members has the right to express opinions on behalf of the society.

If you wish to learn more about Mensa and how to take the Mensa Entrance Test, write for details to one of the addresses below. We are sure that if you are successful you will derive a great deal of enjoyment and mental stimulation from membership of the society.

UK

British Mensa Ltd
Mensa House
St John's Square
Wolverhampton
WV2 4AH

INTERNATIONAL

Mensa International Ltd
15 The Ivories
6–8 Northampton Street
London
N1 2HY

USA

American Mensa Ltd
2626 E14 Street
Brooklyn
NY 11235

AUSTRALIA

Australian Mensa
16 Elliot Avenue
Carnegie
Victoria 3163

ABOUT THE PUZZLES

So that you can monitor your performance we have allocated one of the following star ratings to each puzzle:

★ Standard
★★ More challenging
★★★ Difficult
★★★★ Incredibly difficult

You will see that each puzzle has been cross-referenced with two numbers – a question number (Q) and an answer number (A). This has enabled us to mix up the answers section so that there is no risk of your seeing the answer before you tackle the next puzzle.

Happy solving and have fun!

A prolific British puzzle compiler of the 1930s and 1940s, Hubert Philips (Caliban), once wrote that 'a quiz should serve to give pleasure to those who take part in it: it is not an examination'. All our books are compiled in this spirit and are meant to be a leisurely diversion from life's more pressing problems.

Our first section is a puzzle pot pourri to prepare your mind for what is to follow and perhaps to give you some insight into the way our minds work.

Q1	★/★★/★★★	A34

Letter Sequences

1. ★ What is the next letter in the sequence
F, S, T, F ?

2. ★★★ What letter completes the sequence
S, O, E, N, S, Y ?

3. ★★ What is next in the sequence
A, B, G, D, E ?

4. ★★ What is the next letter in the sequence
C, B, R, R, C ?

5. ★★ What is the next letter in the sequence
F, A, J, N, S, A, D, J ?

Keywords

1. I am eight letters long – 12345678.
   My 1234 is an atmospheric condition.
   My 34567 supports a plant.
   My 4567 is to appropriate.
   My 45 is a friendly thank-you.
   My 678 is a canny name.
   What am I?

2. I am seven letters long – 1234567.
   My 123 is a vehicle.
   My 2345 was a pop group.
   My 456 is a piece of luggage.
   My 567 is a period of time.
   What am I?

3. I am nine letters long – 123456789.
   My 123 is a mischief.
   My 3456 is to the left.
   My 678 is a shade of brown.
   My 789 is a social insect.
   What am I?

Q3 ★ A21

The Knight's Tour

Find the correct starting point and then, by the knight's tour, spell out the message. The knight moves as in chess – see diagram below.

BE	ARE	OF	FUN	TEASERS
SIMPLE	MUCH	CAN	COMING	SOLVING
PEOPLE	IN	REALIZE	MATHS	THERE
HOW	LITTLE	MORE	THE	TO

	X		X	
X				X
		K		
X				X
	X		X	

Q4 ★ A25

Four Teasers

1. 'How much is this bag of potatoes?' asked the man. '32lb divided by half its own weight,' said the shopkeeper. How much did the bag of potatoes weigh?

2. A workman was repairing telephone boxes that had been vandalized in the town centre. The chief engineer said: 'See those 12 boxes in a line over there? Well, seven out of the first nine are broken. Go and mend one of them.' The workman went straight to number nine. How did he know that one was broken?

3. A tramp collected cigarette ends until he had 1728. How many cigarettes in total could he make and smoke from these if 12 cigarette ends make up one cigarette?

4. What is the next letter in the sequence

D, H, M, S?

Q5	★ ★	A121

Letters

Where would you insert the letters D and K in the grid?

G	M		J
B	L	E	O
I	C	N	H
P	F		A

Q6	★ ★ ★	A13

Riddle

You are looking for a one-word answer to this riddle.

Leave the tea and get me a pot,
And I'll devise a devious plot.
Ideas are fixed firmly in my mind,
As I lay in my bed, my thoughts entwined,
I cannot sleep, so I take a drink,
Breathe in the air, I'm on the brink.
This story will be the best seller yet,
The sweet smell of success I'll surely get.

Q7 ★★ A42

Logic

Use logical deduction to determine which letter should replace the ?.

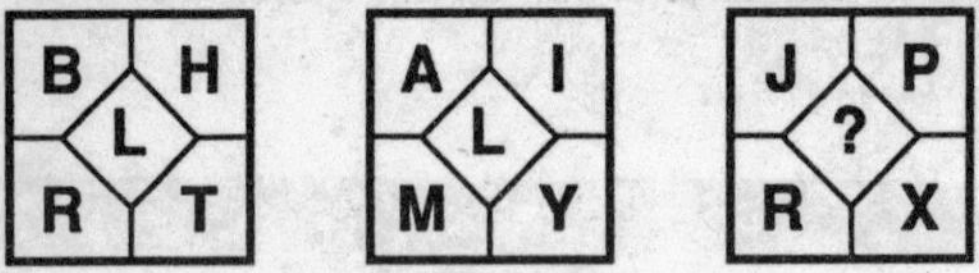

Q8 ★★ A52

Find the Number

Find the correct starting point and work from square to square, horizontally, vertically and diagonally, to spell out a number. The letters that are not used can be arranged to form the Roman numeral value of the number spelled out.

L	H	E	U	H	M
U	N	S	X	O	T
N	N	I	A	O	Y
D	D	N	W	T	M
D	R	N	D	T	R
E	A	C	F	O	M

Letter Change

Change one letter from each word in every group to make, in each case, a well-known phrase. For example, Pet rice quack will become Get rich quick.

1. Bust she joy
2. Run any dames
3. Is lull dry
4. So life I dread
5. Rub sings bound
6. Toots any sail
7. Slow hit end cord
8. Plan in works
9. Hike any seem
10. Plan wits fine
11. Tame if mood tart
12. Burn o dead jar
13. Same toe say
14. Odd gives take
15. Wish oven army
16. On she ran
17. Put on older
18. Life end lot five
19. Let I love in
20. And odd cow

ODD ONE OUT

In the puzzles in this section your task is to find one good reason, over and above all others, why one of the options given is the odd one out. You will have to put your mind to work to explore all the possibilities and use a great deal of lateral thinking.

To try to give you some inkling into the way our minds work on this type of puzzle, we have devised the unusual example illustrated here, which we call 'added difficulty'. In part 1, of the five letters shown – A, D, D, E and D – which is the odd one out? Our answer is A because it has lateral symmetry. In other words, if a line were drawn down the centre from top to bottom the left side of the letter would be identical to the right side. The other letters have vertical symmetry –

1. **ADDED**

2.

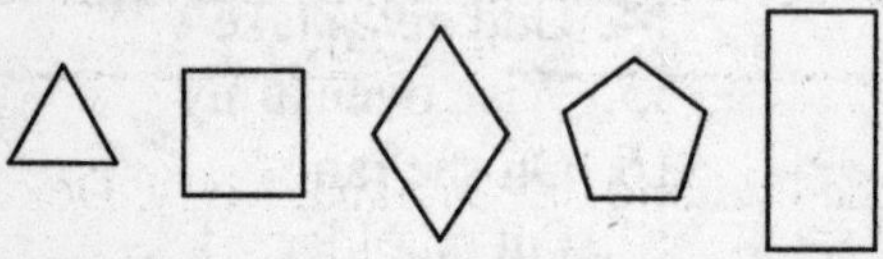

3.

i.e., a line drawn across the middle from left to right will reveal identical top and bottom halves.

In part 2 the odd one out is the far right-hand figure (the rectangle) because all the other figures have identical sides.

The real difficulty begins in part 3. Which is the odd one out here? The reason cannot be the same as in parts 1 and 2. It cannot be argued that the figure containing the letter A is the odd one out because the letter A is laterally symmetrical, because you could equally argue that the last figure is the odd one out because its sides are unequal. If one of these figures is still the odd one out, it has to be because of something entirely different involving the marriage of letter and figure.

Can you work out the logic and discover which of the five figures is the odd one out? (See A26.)

Q10 ★★ A59

Find the Lady

Who is the odd one out – Diana, Mary, Deirdre or Carol?

Q11 ★ A3

Nine-letter Words

Which is the odd one out?

Telephone

Limousine

Freighter

Driftwood

Q12 ★★★ A62

Odd One Out

Which is the odd one out?

Q13 ★★ A35

Nonsense Sentences

Which of the following nonsense sentences is the odd one out?

1. More solo goals

2. Lame animal pairs

3. Only some sail

4. Plaza mail louse

Q14 ★ A22

Letters and Numerals

Which is the odd one out?

50YN10

100E500AR

E50AN500

100AME50

5050A1000A

BU5050

Q15 ★★ A10

Odd One Out

Which is the odd one out?

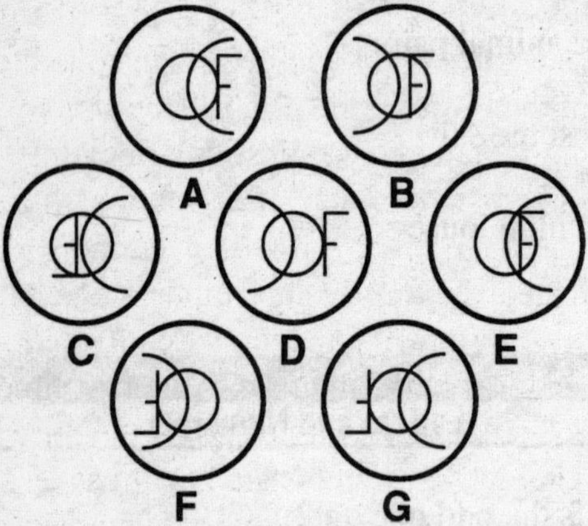

CRYPTOGRAPHY

Cryptography is the system of writing messages in codes or ciphers. A cryptogram is the coded message, and cryptanalysis is the breaking of the codes or cipher without the key.

The simplest cryptograms are those in which each letter of the alphabet from A to Z (the plain text) is substituted for another in the coded text – for example F for H or B for T.

Another method is to substitute randomly chosen numbers for each letter – for example, 56 may stand for E or 29 for K. In even more complicated versions of such ciphers one letter may have more than one number equivalent – for example, the letter E may be 29 the first time it appears, 36 the second time and 21 the third time. These alternative numbers are known as homophones. Without the key such messages, and even more complicated variations of them, would be virtually impossible to decode except by intelligence departments with sophisticated equipment.

In this section we include several different types of cryptogram that have been developed throughout history, each of which will present its own demanding challenge.

Q16 ★ A76

The Polybius Cipher

This code is based on a cipher invented by a Greek writer, Polybius, in the second century BC. Can you work out the system and decipher the quotation below?

A	B	C	D	E
F	G	H	IJ	K
L	M	N	O	P
Q	R	S	T	U
V	W	X	Y	Z

44,23,15 52,34,42,31,14,43

22,42,15,11,44 32,15,33

23,11,51,15 33,34,44

13,34,32,32,34,33,31,54

12,15,15,33 22,42,15,11,44

43,13,23,34,31,11,42,43 33,34,42

24,44,43 22,42,15,11,44

43,13,23,34,31,11,42,43

22,42,15,11,44 32,15,33

34,31,24,51,15,42

52,15,33,14,15,31,31

23,34,31,32,15,43

Q17 ★★ A68

The Caesar Alphabet

This simple code was used by Julius Caesar when writing secret messages to his allies. Can you crack the system and decode the quotation?

YJJ ZYB NPCACBCLRQ ZCEYL

YQ HSQRGDGYZJC KCYQSPCQ

Q18 ★ A53

Three-letter Words

The Greek philosopher Pythagoras described three as the perfect number – it has a beginning, a middle and an end. The three-letter words below hide a familiar saying. Can you crack the code to reveal the saying?

mob, log, car, ego, ape, fro, wee, beg, jar, tap, foe,

toy, oil, sun, ear, emu, ill, hub, our, awe

Q19 ★★★★ A43

The Hidden Message

Can you find a hidden message in the memo below?

```
James is insisting that
the second key to the
office supplies cabinet,
and the two coloured
transparencies, will
first need clearance
before Kenneth and
Philip arrive at the
office to check all the
material early next
Monday, so that Peter
can develop them on
Tuesday afternoon and
take them round to
David's department on
Wednesday morning.
```

Cryptosymbol

Decode the following quotation.

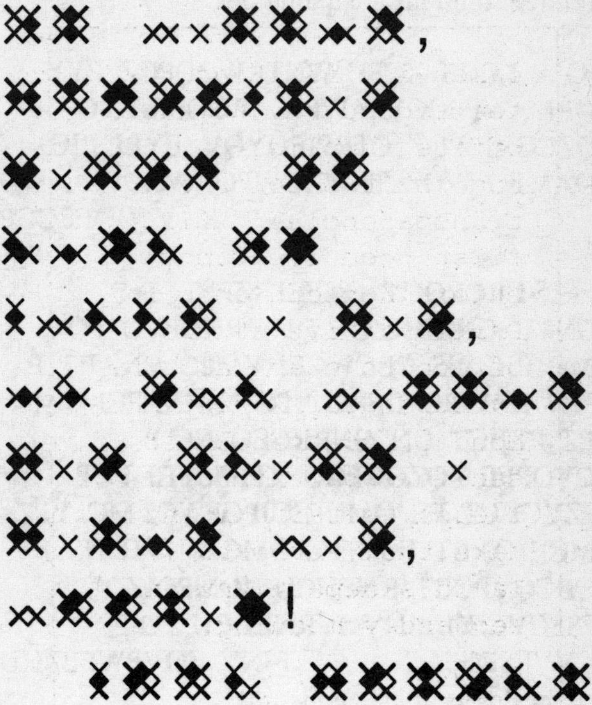

Three Cryptograms

Each cryptogram is a straight substitution code, where one letter of the alphabet has been replaced by another. Each of the three is in a different code. All three solutions are quotations.

1. O'A LCGS XCFF WNTRWOQPCZ PYY XOPJ AWPPCGV AWPJCAWPONWF, O RQZCGVPWQZ CTRWPOYQV, EYPJ PJC VOAMFC WQZ TRWZGWPONWF.

X. V. UOFECGP

2. F VCRCRQCV QCFEJ MPETCT P ZGNVC GNRXNZCT QU *RNDPVO PO OMC PJC NS CBCWCE. YMPO GNABT F ZPU? F SCBO BFHC *TC *HNNEFEJ YMN YPZ PZHCT ON GNRRCEO NE P GCVOPFE PQZOVPGO XPFEOFEJ PET PEZYCVCT FE OMC ECJPOFWC. MC YPZ OMCE ONBT FO YPZ OMC YNVH NS P GCBCQVPOCT RNEHCU. 'OMPO'Z TFSSCVCEO. SNV P RNEHCU FO'Z OCVVFSFG.'

FJNV ZOVPWFEZHU

(* indicates a capitalized word)

3. JN PJC VBOMUH GAACZUOYT XC NRNZK FGY'H GUROAN ROMM JGRN G AZCCDNU JCBHN.

UGYOHJ SZCRNZV

Q22 ★ ★ ★ A86

Cryptokey 1

Start by solving the cryptogram that follows which is a straightforward code in which each letter of the alphabet has been replaced by another.

FNHG LVNGK; N QOW'F, FSGD QXHG IOKF OF KJQS NZZGMJVOZ NWFGZAOVK

Now try to find a keyed phrase (6, 5) connected with the cryptogram. Against each letter of plain text (column 1) write its encoded form (column 2). Then, against each letter of code text (column 3) write its plain text form (column 4). You will find that some of column 4 is in alphabetical order; the letters that are not are those making up the key phrase. They appear in their correct order, but, of course, repeated letters have been omitted and must be replaced. A little imagination is needed to work out the hidden phrase – for instance, ANPLEDY would be all that would appear of 'an apple a day'.

1	2	3	4
A		A	
B		B	
C		C	
D		D	
E		E	
F		F	
G		G	
H		H	
I		I	
J		J	
K		K	
L		L	
M		M	
N		N	
O		O	
P		P	
Q		Q	
R		R	
S		S	
T		T	
U		U	
V		V	
W		W	
X		X	
Y		Y	
Z		Z	

Q23 ★ ★ ★ A95

Cryptokey 2

1	2	3	4
A		A	
B		B	
C		C	
D		D	
E		E	
F		F	
G		G	
H		H	
I		I	
J		J	
K		K	
L		L	
M		M	
N		N	
O		O	
P		P	
Q		Q	
R		R	
S		S	
T		T	
U		U	
V		V	
W		W	
X		X	
Y		Y	
Z		Z	

Using the same rules as in Q22, decode the following, then find a keyed phrase (5, 6, 3, 3).

SKTOT SGR WQTLS RQWLMXOLSXRMO RV SKT *TMWAXOK OCTLZXMW NTBRPQLPXTO SKT *UQXSXOK *TBCXQT LMN SKT *EMXSTN *OSLSTO, GXAA KLFT SR UT ORBTGKLS BXHTN EC SRWTSKTQ XM ORBT RV SKTXQ LVVLXQO... X NR MRS FXTG SKT CQRPTOO GXSK LMI BXOWXFXMWO. X PREAN MRS OSRC XS XV X GXOKTN; MR RMT PLM OSRC XS. AXZT SKT *BXOOXOOXCCX, XS YEOS ZTTCO QRAAXMW LARMW. ATS XS QRAA. ATS XS QRAA RM VEAA VARRN, XMTHRQLUAT, XQQTOXOSXUAT UTMXWMLMS, SR UQRLNTQ ALMNO LMN UTSSTQ NLIO.

GXMOSRM PKEQPKXAA

(* indicates a capitalized word)

WORD GAMES

Words are like leaves; and where they most abound,
Much fruit of sense beneath is rarely found.

Alexander Pope

To have mastery over words is to have in one's possession the ability to produce order out of chaos. To a certain extent a puzzle compiler is a creator of chaos and is throwing out a challenge to the solver to sort out the chaos and to restore order – in other words, to find the solution that has in some way been disguised.

All the puzzles in this section involve finding words from the grids or clues provided, and each provides its own different type of challenge.

Synchronized Synonyms

Each grid contains the letters of eight eight-letter words. All the letters are in the correct order, and each letter is used once only. Each word in Grid A has a synonym in Grid B, and the letters of each of the eight pairs of synonyms are in exactly the same position in each grid. Clues to each pair of synonyms are given below the grids in no particular order.

Example – the answers to the clue 'Crack' are the words 'Fracture' in Grid A and 'Splinter' in Grid B.

GRID A

M	J	A	F	P	I	D	R
E	(F)	E	R	A	R	M	E
T	A	S	(R)	P	E	D	U
F	(A)	O	D	I	I	V	I
E	A	B	S	F	(C)	U	(T)
N	L	M	(U)	T	I	A	B
C	L	T	I	(R)	I	L	E
E	E	L	E	E	N	(E)	G

GRID B

R	I	P	W	P	M	G	R
O	(S)	U	R	R	H	A	O
E	U	K	(P)	J	O	L	M
I	(L)	E	M	T	I	M	A
A	L	B	S	E	(I)	S	(N)
T	L	O	(T)	N	N	A	G
C	U	T	T	(E)	U	R	E
E	E	H	E	E	I	(R)	C

Clues:

Crack
Contemplate
August
Subterfuge
Foreword
Childish
Viable
Macabre

Jumble

Commencing always with the centre letter A spell out eight 11-letter words. You may travel in any direction – horizontal, vertical or diagonal – but each letter must be used only once.

R	U	N	U	I	M	A	T	E
E	T	C	P	X	O	O	N	E
N	O	I	U	P	R	L	C	Y
B	A	T	C	P	L	T	I	C
O	R	P	P	A	N	T	E	R
M	N	R	R	R	L	T	A	N
E	G	I	A	C	L	E	I	V
N	T	A	C	H	L	G	O	E
Y	L	L	I	A	A	C	I	R

Q26 ★★ A28

Square

Divide the square into four identical sections. Each section must contain the same nine letters, which can be arranged into a familiar nine-letter word.

H	L	U	B	A	E
E	L	A	G	G	A
B	B	U	L	L	A
A	A	A	U	H	L
U	L	G	A	E	B
H	L	G	E	H	L

Q27 ★ A77

Square Words

Work clockwise around the perimeter and finish at the centre square to spell the six nine-letter words. You have to provide the missing letters. The six words you are looking for are three pairs of synonyms.

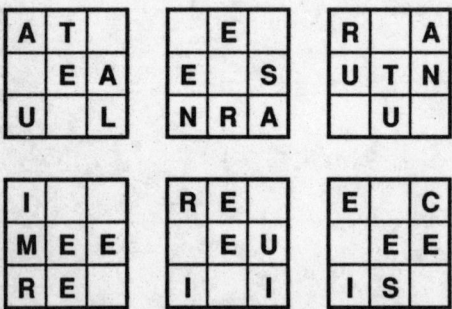

A	T	
	E	A
U		L

	E	
E		S
N	R	A

R		A
U	T	N
	U	

I		
M	E	E
R	E	

R	E	
	E	U
I		I

E		C
	E	E
I	S	

Q28 ★ ★ ★ A116

Pyramid Word

Solve the five clues, enter the correct words in the pyramid and then re-arrange all the letters to find a 15-letter word.

The Roman numeral for 50 (1)
At home (2)
Came face to face (3)
Oxidation (4)
A person of exceptional holiness (5)

Q29 ★ ★ A12

No-repeat Letters

The grid contains 25 different letters. What is the longest word that can be found by starting anywhere and working from square to square, horizontally, vertically or diagonally, and not repeating a letter?

Y	K	C	H	V
P	M	L	I	G
J	O	A	U	N
B	F	R	Q	E
S	W	D	T	X

Q30 ★★ A45

Word Construction

Use each of the 30 small words below once only to construct 10 words. There are three small words in each word.

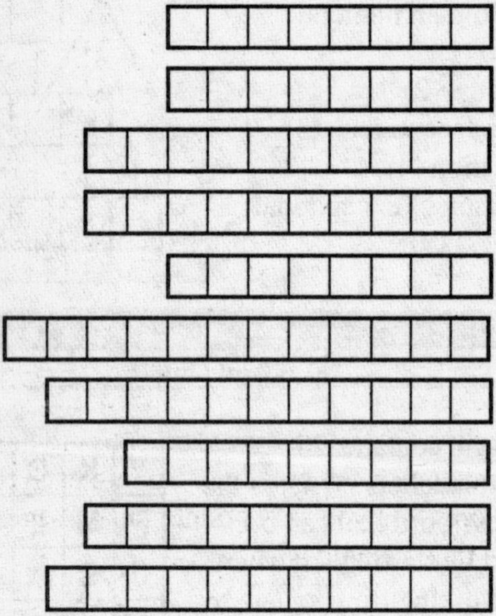

IN FAT BOUND WARD LEAGUE
KITCHEN ATE OUR BE AND UP
DISC HER BAR FAN LAND OWL
MEAD RED ICE POLL OUT ART
TRY CUE IF IN SO AGE BE

Q31 ★ ★ ★ A108

Pyramids

1. Spell out a 15-letter word by entering the pyramid one room at a time. Go into each room once only, but you may go into the passage as many times as you wish.

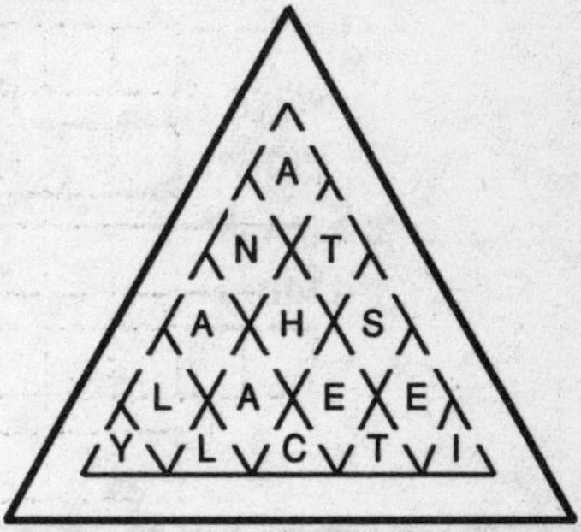

2. Spell out a 15-letter word by entering the pyramid one room at a time. Go into each room once only, but you may go into the passage as many times as you wish.

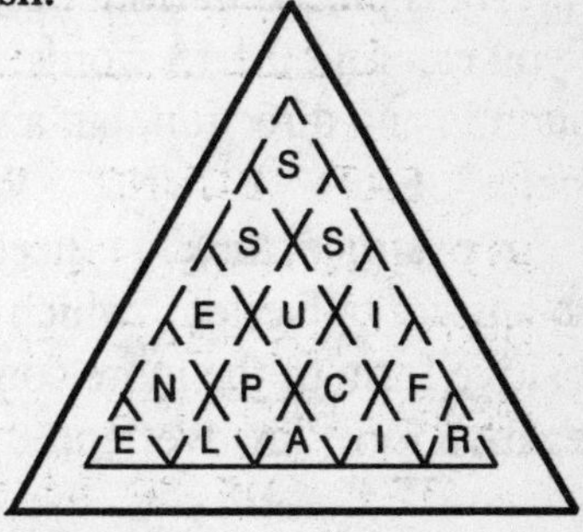

Q32 ★★ A88

Categorize

Arrange the following words into four groups of three.

Barge	Beat
Hammer	Hike
Mark	Pound
Punt	Slog
Smack	Thrash
Tramp	Trek

Q33 ★★★ A96

Word Search

Hidden in the word square are 15 words that are rarely used in their positive form and that are better known in their negative form, usually when a prefix is placed in front of the positive word. See if you can find the 15 words. The words can be found in any direction, but always in a straight line.

For example, the clue 'heedful' would produce the answer 'advertent' which is the less often used positive form of the more commonly used negative form 'inadvertent'.

E	N	I	M	A	T	S	I	H	T
L	V	E	L	B	A	F	F	E	N
B	T	I	Y	Y	L	T	T	H	A
I	P	B	T	D	N	A	N	T	T
G	M	L	I	A	L	N	I	U	C
I	E	O	R	O	B	E	A	O	E
R	K	O	S	U	T	L	I	C	F
R	D	N	O	R	F	I	E	W	N
O	O	L	I	C	I	T	C	A	I
C	T	N	E	T	R	E	V	D	A

Positive–form clues:

1. Heedful
2. An agent of infection
3. Crystalline base affects allergic reactions
4. Correctable
5. Avoidable
6. An odorous substance
7. Comforted
8. Manageable
9. Free from weird qualities
10. Relating to life
11. Marked by finesse
12. Capable of being expressed
13. Trim
14. Allowable
15. Secure to a staff

Hexagon

Fit the following words into the six spaces around the appropriate number on the diagram so that each word correctly interlinks with the two words on either side – you will see that each word has two consecutive letters in common with the word next to it.

Note: to arrive at the correct solution you will have to enter some words clockwise and some anticlockwise.

RECESS
REVOKE
SENSOR
REMOTE
DEVOUT
LANCER
SOLVED
TENDER
PLANET
ROUTED
TENNER
DETOUR

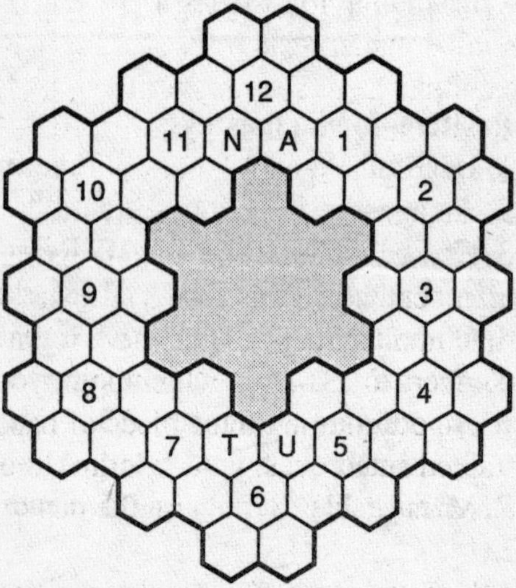

KICKSELF

Lewis Carroll had a favourite trick that he enjoyed trying out on his friends. We have used the same trick many times. It never fails to amaze, and we have yet to find anyone who has worked out how it is done. We will take you through the trick stage by stage. First, you write a four-figure number on a piece of paper – for example, 3144 as shown – your 'victim' is then invited to write another four-figure number underneath – for example, he or she may write down 7564. You then write another four-figure number beneath this – i.e., 2435. Next your 'victim' writes down another number of his or her choice, in this case 3712, and you add the final number, 6287. Then the 'victim' totals up the numbers to 23142, at which point you reach into your pocket, bring out a piece of paper folded and stapled and request your 'victim' to open it up. Needless to say, written on the paper is the number 23142.

3144
7564
2435
3712
6287
23142

Can you work out how this is done? It is a first-class kickself puzzle (See A27).

Q35 ★ A44

Equation

Correct the following equation by freely moving the given four digits but without adding any mathematical symbols.

26 = 47

Q36 ★ A113

Strike Out

Strike out 10 letters to reveal a short phrase.

ATSEHNLOERTPTHTREARSES

Q37 ★★ A11

The Magic 11

Insert the 36 numbers into the grid in such a way that the same number does not appear in any horizontal or vertical line more than once and the six-figure numbers produced in each horizontal, vertical and corner-to-corner line can be divided exactly by 11 when read either forwards or backwards.

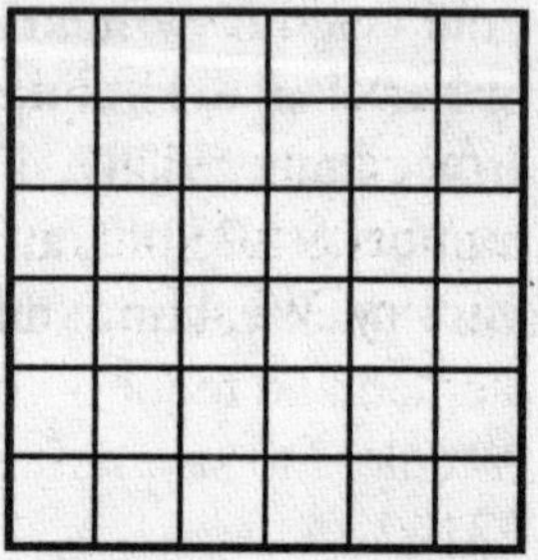

111111 222222
444444 555555
777777 888888

Q38 ★ ★ ★ A110

Calculation

If these two numbers total 8679, what do the two numbers below total?

8159 + 1912

6128 + 9091

Q39 ★ ★ A87

Work It Out

I take what has been projected upwards by a member of the Talpidae family and, in a very short time, create what a major orogeny has taken centuries to produce during the earth's geological history. What am I doing?

Rebuses

A rebus is an arrangement of letters or symbols that is used to indicate a word or phrase; for example, bbbbbbbbbb = beeline. What are the following well-known phrases?

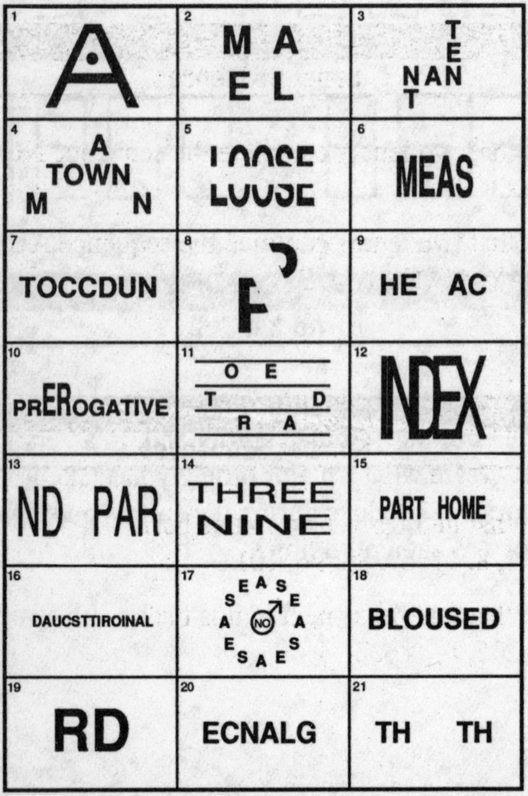
1
A
2
M A
E L
3
T E NAN T
4
A
TOWN
M N
5
LOOSE
LOOSE
6
MEAS
7
TOCCDUN
8
9
HE AC
10
PRERROGATIVE
11
O E
T D
R A
12
NDEX
13
ND PAR
14
THREE
NINE
15
PART HOME
16
DAUCSTTIROINAL
17
EASESAEASEASA
NO
18
BLOUSED
19
RD
20
ECNALG
21
TH TH

Q41 ★★★ A8

Lewis

If Lewis was driving a Volkswagen car with the number plate ML8ML8, what model is the car and what colour is it?

Q42 ★★ A72

Letter Sequences

1. What two letters complete the sequence NLN, RLN, CTAD?

2. What two letters continue the sequence AUR, ERAY, AC, PI, A, UE?

Q43 ★ A70

Number Sequences

1. What number is next in this list?
0, 1, 8, 11, 69, 88, 96, 101

2. What number is next in this list?
1, 2, 5, 8, 11, 22

DIAGRAMS

The type of diagrammatic tests in this section are known as 'culture fair' tests, and they are widely used in intelligence testing. Their advantage is that they use logic instead of word knowledge, and they are thus more accessible to all members of the community. These tests are considered to be just as reliable as verbal tests, because spatial understanding and logical reasoning are a good guide to levels of intelligence.

If at first you are baffled by these puzzles, stick at them. Even if you cannot work out the answer at the first attempt, it may suddenly click into place if you take a fresh look later.

Q44 ★★ A80

Peaks

Cut the figure into two identical parts.

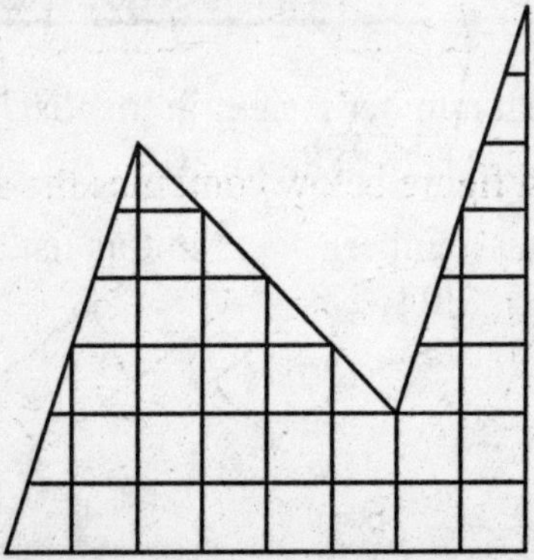

Q45 ★ A31

Analogy

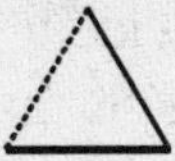 is to  as

 is to

A B C D E

Q46 ★ ★ A79

Logic

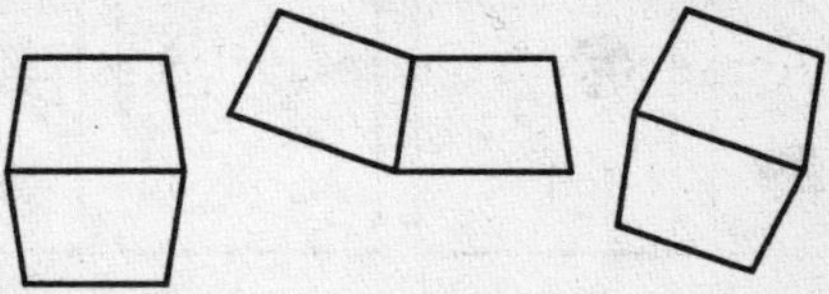

Which figure below continues the above sequence?

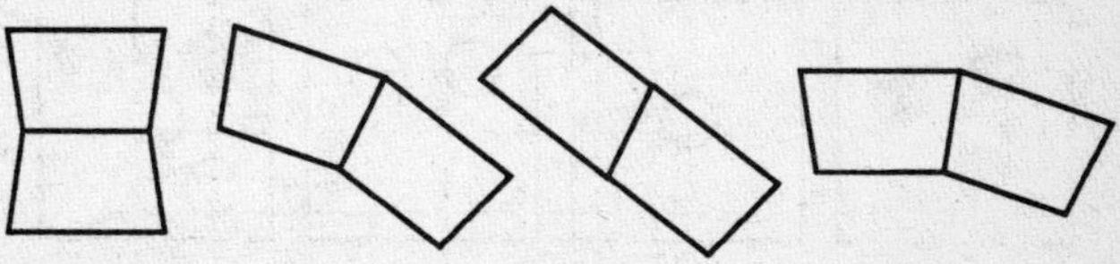

A B C D

Q47 ★★★★ A99

Missing Square

Find the missing square.

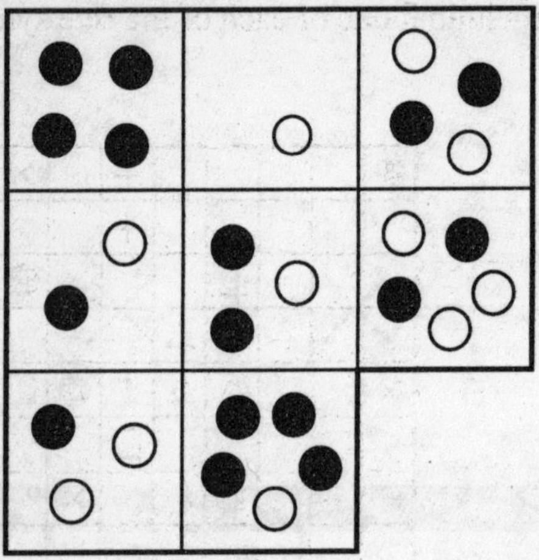

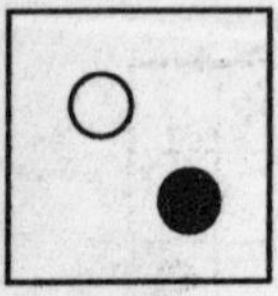

A

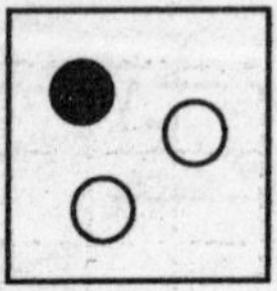

B

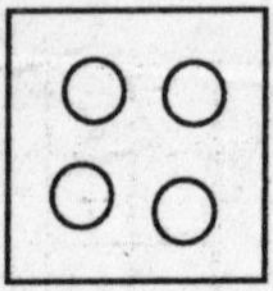

C

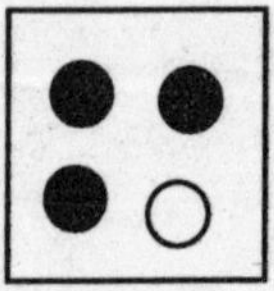

D

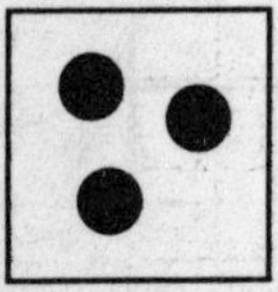

E

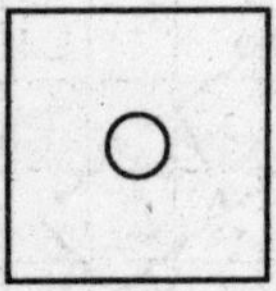

F

G

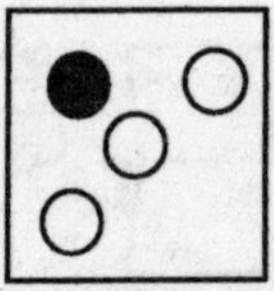

H

Q48 ★★ A112

Symbols

Divide each square into four equal portions, each of which will be the same size and shape and will include within it one of each of the five symbols.

1.

●					+		×
					+		
			□				●
×			△	△			
×			△	△		●	□
	□				□		
	+	+	●			×	

2.

				△		×	
	+			△			
							●
		□		□			●
+	□				□		
			×		+	+	
	●		△	△			
×	●						×

Q49 ★★ A7

Sequence

Which of the options – A, B, C, D or E – continues this sequence?

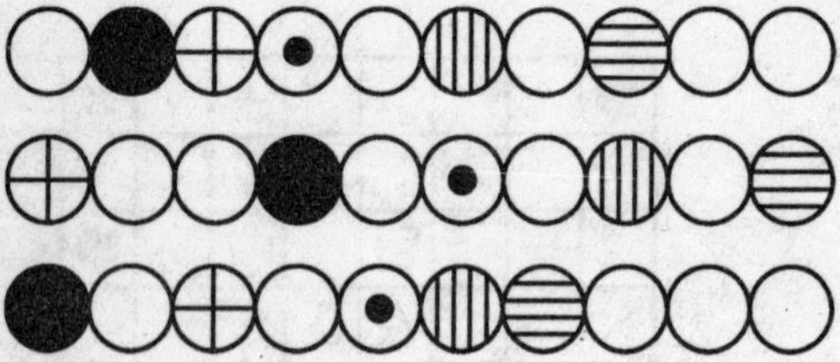

A 

B 

C 

D 

E 

Q50 ★ A98

Dots

What comes next in this sequence, A, B, C, D or E?

A B C D E

Q51 ★★★ A30

Jigsaw Puzzle

How many different symmetrical figures can be formed by fitting together all the pieces below?

Because pieces can be turned over, you will need to trace and cut out the pieces.

Q52 ★ A15

Advance Matrix

Which circle – A, B, C, D, E, F or G – will complete the sequence?

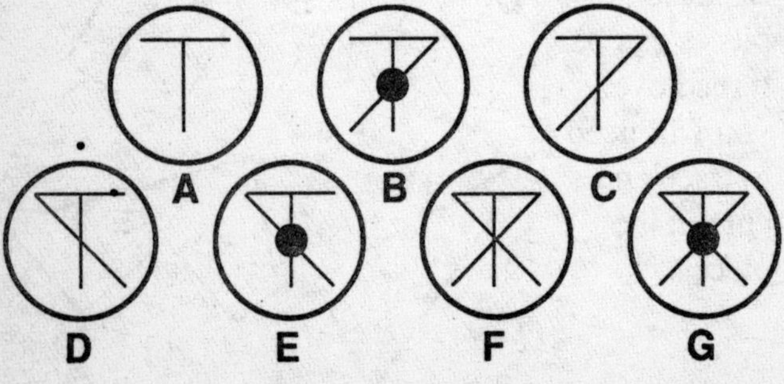

Discs

Which disc – A, B, C, D or E – should come next?

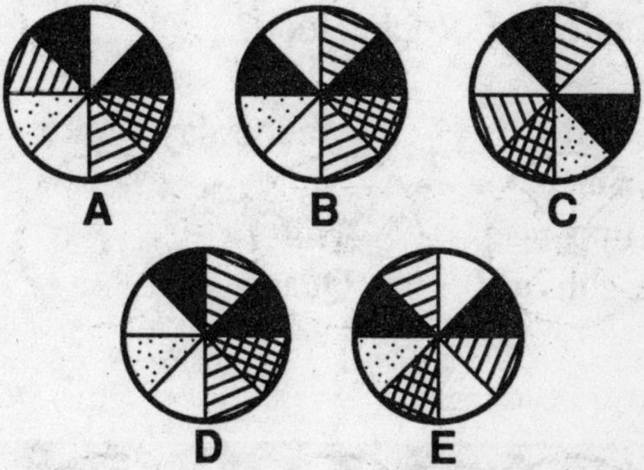

SOMETHING IN COMMON

In these puzzles all the options given have a strong unifying theme. Again, lateral thinking and flexibility of thought are necessary to enable you to start finding the right answers.

Q54 ★★★ A89

Words

What do the following words have in common with Socrates and Robin Hood?

Quarter	Wednesday
Printer	Nutty
Tuppence	Thirty
Lightning	Quarry

Q55 ★★ A69

Peoples

What do the people of Belgium have in common with the people of Bangladesh?

Q56 ★ A101
Common Clues

What do all the following clues have in common?

1. Foam-crested waves
2. A type of small, very faint, dense star
3. A flag of the Royal Navy
4. A useless possession
5. A high pitch of excitement
6. A termite
7. One who gives financial support in a difficult situation
8. The beluga
9. A pardonable misstatement
10. A government report

Q57 ★★ A14
Five Words

What do these five words have in common?

Gorge
Funfair
Feminine
Pendent
Besiege

Q58 ★ A111

Famous Names

What have the following in common?

Raleigh
Bismarck
Columbus
Lincoln
Montgomery

Q59 ★ A29

Seven Clues

What links the following clues?

1. Subject to sudden nose spasms
2. Short medic
3. Ill-tempered
4. Content
5. Inclination to slumber
6. Shy
7. Half-asleep

Q60 ★★ A117

Who's Who

What do the following have in common?

1. A drugged drink
2. Someone who indulges in fantasies
3. A forced selection when there is no alternative
4. A flat round cake
5. The bottom of the sea
6. A man of high fashion
7. A military officer's wide belt
8. A theatre award in the United States
9. A type of petrol bomb
10. A club for elderly people

Q61 ★ A71

What's the Connection?

What do a melon, the city of Tokyo and Ronald have in common?

Q62 ★ ★ A107

What's the Link

What do the answers to the following clues have in common?

1. A departure
2. Amounts
3. Arbiters
4. Pity
5. Rulers
6. Records of events
7. Piece of work
8. Traditional sayings
9. A visible impression
10. A disclosing of information

Q63 ★ ★ ★ A120

Shortbread and Shooting Stars

What have the following in common?

1. Dresden china
2. Shooting stars
3. Shortbread
4. Jumping bean
5. Lead pencil
6. Bald eagle
7. Horned toads
8. Firefly
9. Prairie dog
10. Catgut

NUMBERS

'He uses statistics as a drunken man uses a lamp-post – for support rather than for illumination.'

Andrew Lang

Numbers can be interesting and challenging. They are often confusing, and they are sometimes manipulated and misrepresented, but at the end of the day mathematics is an exact science, and there is only one correct solution to a correctly set calculation or puzzle.

In this book, as in our other books in this series, we have included a number of magic squares because these are of great interest to us. First developed by the ancient Chinese, they are arrays of consecutive numbers in which all rows, columns and diagonals add up to the same total. The most famous of these is the order-3 'lo-shu', which uses the numbers 1–9 once each only to form a 3 x 3 magic square in which each horizontal, vertical and corner-to-corner line totals 15. Do you remember how this square is constructed? (See A83.) The 'lo-shu' is unique because there is only one possible solution – not counting rotations or reflections, of course, of which there are seven additional versions. As the order of magic squares increases, so do the number of different possible versions – for example, not counting rotations and reflections, there are 880 order-4 squares and over 275 million order-5 squares!

There is a formula for working out the sum of the rows of each magic square. To obtain the constant of a standard order-4 square, add the integers from 1 to 16 and divide the sum by 4 – the constant is 34. The constant of an order five square is the sum of the numbers 1 to 25 divided by 5 – i.e., 65. A further simple formula is that the constant = ½ x (order cubed + order). Therefore, for an order-6 square the constant is (6x6x6) + 6 divided by 2 = 111.

Before you tackle the puzzles that follow, here is one additional gentle warm up magic-square puzzle. The grid below contains the numbers 1 to 16 once each only, but alas only five of the lines add up to 34. Your task is to divide the square into four equal-shaped sections and then to re-assemble the four sections to form a true magic square in which each horizontal, vertical and corner-to-corner line totals 34. (See A118.)

13	7	10	4
15	2	12	5
8	9	3	14
1	11	6	16

Q64 ★ ★ ★ A18

Magic Square

Insert the remaining numbers from 1 to 25 to form a magic square in which each horizontal, vertical and corner-to-corner line totals 65.

				15
10				
	5			
		25		
			20	

Q65 ★ ★ ★ A119

The Square Series

What connection do square numbers have with the series 1, 4, 9, 7, 7, 9, 4, 1, 9?

Q66 ★ ★ A102

Athletes

At the athletic meeting, Britain beat Rumania by 35 points to 31. Under a new scoring system, Britain took four first places, three second places and one third place. How many events were there and how were the points for first , second and third places allocated?

Q67 ★★ A33

Square Numbers

Can you find the lowest nine-digit square number that uses the digits 1 to 9 once each only, and then find the highest square number to use the same nine digits?

Q68 ★★★★ A106

One Hundred

Therc are 11 ways of expressing the number 100 as a number and fraction using the nine digits once each only. For example,

91+ 5823/647 = 100

How many of the other 10 ways can you find? Nine of the ways involve the use of a number above 80 (as shown in the example above, which uses the number 91); one way involves the use of a number less than 10.

Q69 ★★★★ A74

Day Finder

On which day of the week will 31 December 1999 fall? Calculate it without looking at a calender.

Q70 ★ ★ ★ A47

Connections

Insert the numbers 0 to 10 in the circles so that for any particular circle the sum of the numbers in the circles connected directly to it equals the value corresponding to the number in that circle as given in the list below.

Example
1=14 (4+7+3)
4=8 (7+1)
7=5 (4+1)
3=1

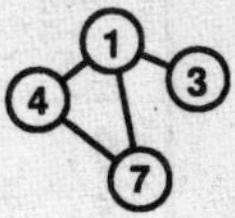

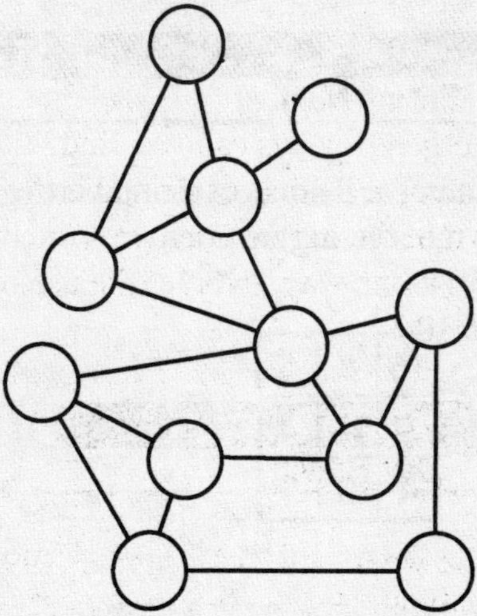

0 = 21
1 = 19
2 = 25
3 = 16
4 = 2
5 = 30
6 = 4
7 = 11
8 = 6
9 = 14
10 = 8

Q71	★ ★ ★	A82

Magic Square

Insert the remaining numbers from 1 to 25 to form a magic square in which each horizontal, vertical and corner-to-corner line totals 65.

				15
	5			
			20	
10				
		25		

Q72	★ ★	A17

Missing Number

Study the numbers in each horizontal and vertical line and work out the missing number.

15	8	5
4	15	4
4	5	?

Why is AH, SPOTTING HOT NEWS a particularly appropriate phrase? (See A1.)

Invented by the Greek poet Lycophron in AD280, anagrams have been popular throughout history. The best ones are those in which the re-arranged letters bear some relationship to the original – for example, the word INCOMPREHENSIBLE can be arranged into the phrase PROBLEM IN CHINESE; the phrase I AM A PENCIL DOT is an anagram of A DECIMAL POINT; and WINSTON LEONARD SPENCER CHURCHILL is an anagram of AND WE'LL COPE 'N' CRUSH HITLER IN SCORN. One of the compilers of this book describes himself as an ESTIMATING ENIGMATIST.

Before you tackle the anagrams that follow, why not try your hand at compiling an anagram yourself? Between 1804 and 1806 a journey of exploration across the American continent was made by Meriwether Lewis and William Clark. Promoted by Thomas Jefferson, the expedition took the explorers over the Rockies, down the Columbia River to the Pacific and explored the Yellowstone River on the return journey, and went on to establish the American claim to the Louisiana Purchase. It was known as THE LEWIS AND CLARK EXPEDITION. Can you use all these 26 letters once each only to make an appropriate phrase? For our solution (4, 6, 5, 7, 4) see A32.

Q73 ★ A46

Reverse Anagram

If we presented you with the words MAR, AM and FAR and asked you to find the smallest word that contained all the letters from which these words could be produced, we would expect you to come up with the word FARM. Here is a further list of words: CHAIR, CLAY, CARD and CRUSH. What is the smallest word from which all these four words can be produced?

Q74 ★ ★ ★ A81

Anagrammed Phrases

Each of the following is an anagram of a well-known phrase, for example:

OIL SHIPS TART = TO SPLIT HAIRS.

1. FASHION BOTTOM CAP
2. SOUR EVERY SIGHT
3. TON IT O GRABBER
4. MILD HIKE GREAT
5. YARK THIRD MAN DOC

Q75 ★ ★ A90
Words

The following are all one-word anagrams

14-letter words
1. Not a stair I mind
2. Hit blue sex gain
3. Crop sender once
4. Promise I rap Pat
5. Need permit rate

15-letter words
1. Note a crime graph
2. His stroppy cheat
3. Export men in a tie
4. Liven cheery mops
5. I start a main toil

Q76 ★ ★ ★ A103
Anagrams

1. VACATE PRO TEM (2 words)
2. CUCKOO TWIRL SCENE (2 words)
3. HE NOTICED HIS COMB WAS ON EDGE (1 word; the anagram is only part of the phrase)

Q77 ★ ★ A93
I'll Make a Wise Phrase

Each of the following is an anagram of a play by Shakespeare.

1. Gear link
2. Listen did cross aura
3. Had a mooning butt, ouch!
4. Solvers all boot us
5. Cheery or frets doom
6. Let the rains wet
7. Cool us rain
8. Adjoin me to rule
9. Fathom tension
10. So I cut and it runs

Q78 ★ ★ **A2**

Spherical

Complete the word in each column. All the words end in S, and the scrambled letters in the section to the right of each column can be arranged to form a word that will give you a clue to the word you are trying to find to fit in the column.

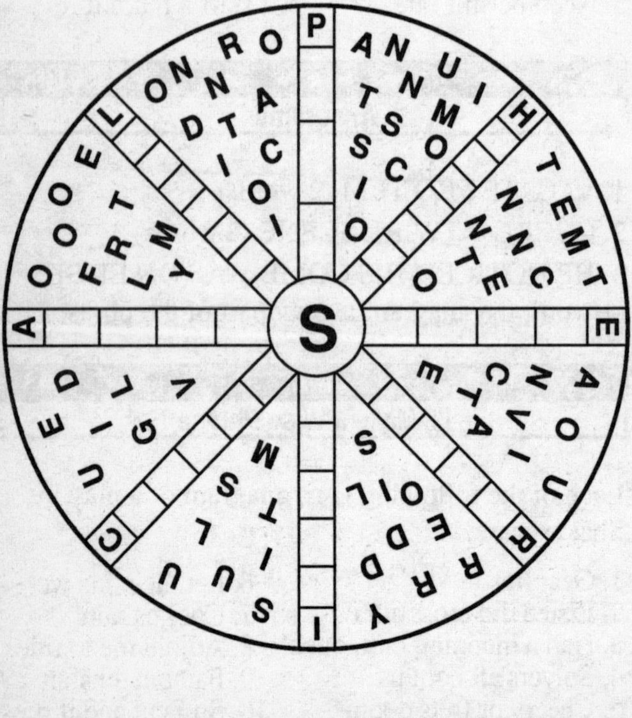

Anagrammed Synonyms

Study the following list of three words. Your task is to find the two out of the three words that can be paired to form an anagram of another word, which is a synonym of the word remaining. For example, in the group LEG – MEEK – NET, the words LEG and NET are an anagram of GENTLE, which is a synonym of the remaining word MEEK.

1. DOTE – GRIT – FRUIT
2. DIVE – MET – LUMP
3. REIN – RIOT – HEART
4. SIP – DIE – HER
5. SOOT – INSIPID – MOOD
6. PAPER – PLAIN – TAN
7. CLIP – LAIR – CUT
8. ROPE – START – PRONE
9. PET – OUR – TEAM
10. CAD – MATE – MORE
11. PLAN – TOP – NICE
12. OLD – TAN – NICE
13. GEMS – SEA – NOTE
14. ATE – URGE – RENT
15. DEED – LONE – REST

Anagram Theme

In each of the following, arrange the 14 words in pairs so that each pair is an anagram of another word or name. The seven words produced will have a linking theme. For example, if the words DIAL and THAN were in the list they could be paired to form an anagram of THAILAND and the theme would be countries.

1. CHIN PIT
   COOL RIP
   CRIB RUN
   CULT SAP
   HALLS SNAP
   HARD TEE
   IS TO

2. ADD HAS
   AGO LID
   APE RACE
   BARN RIM
   BEER RUG
   BUN STAIN
   GLAD TEN

Q81 ★★ A36

Anagrammed Quotation

This quotation from William Wordsworth's ode *Intimations of Immortality* has had 10 words removed, all of which have been anagrammed. Can you solve the 10 anagrams below, which are in no particular order and which are all one-word answers, and then restore them to their correct place in the quotation?

Our noisy tears seem ______ in the being
Of the _____ _____: truths that wake,
To _____ never:
Which _____ _____, nor mad _____,
Nor Man nor Boy,
Nor all that is at _____ with joy,
Can utterly _____ or _____!

1. Tiny me
2. Tom's men
3. Sob hail
4. The rein
5. Stills senses
6. Len's ice
7. He rips
8. Rent ale
9. Red toys
10. Over a dune

'Every production of genius must be the production of enthusiasm.'

Benjamin Disraeli

'Genius is one percent inspiration and ninety-nine percent perspiration.'

Thomas Alva Edison

To solve the selection of puzzles in this section, which have just one thing in common – their fiendishly high degree of difficulty – you will require enthusiasm, inspiration and a certain amount of perspiration.

Q82 ★ ★ ★ ★ A50

An Ancient Fraction

For what purpose did the ancient Chinese use the fraction $^{355}/_{113}$, and how is exactly the same result arrived at by using the integers 3, 7 and 16?

Q83 ★ ★ ★ ★ A55

A Magic '260'

Insert the remaining numbers from 1 to 64 to form a magic square in which each horizontal, vertical and corner-to-corner line totals 260.

	10					15	
				45			
25		35					
40		30					
				20			
	50					55	
			5	60			

Q84 ★ ★ ★ ★ A65

Game Show

You are on a game show and are shown three doors. There is a car behind one door and a goat behind each of the other doors.

You select door number 1, and your chances of finding the car are 2 to 1 against.

The game show host opens door number 2 and reveals a goat. Now your chance of winning the car has reduced to even money.

The host now invites you to change doors to number 3 if you wish. Should you change doors?

Q85 ★ ★ ★ ★ A85

Mathematicians

Six mathematicians sat around a table discussing their ages. Those who were over 40 years of age were truthful unless their ages were a multiple of 17; those who were under 40 years of age lied unless their ages were divisible by 13. None of the mathematicians was over 70 years old. The total of their ages was 261. Each mathematician said:

1. Number 5 is older than I am.
2. Number 1 is 30 years younger than Number 3.
3. I am 51.
4. Number 3 is 52. I am not 29.
5. Number 1 is a prevaricator. Number 6 is 39.
6. Number 4 is wrong. Number 2 is 39.

How old were they?

Q86 ★ ★ ★ A5

Factorial

What is unusual about the number 5913? Clue: try factorials – i.e., 3! = 3 x 2 x 1.

Q87 ★★★★ A61

Stair-rods

'It's raining stair-rods,' said Jim. 'If it were,' said Sid, 'I could use them with this tape measure to calculate the area of that small puddle on the lawn.' What method did Sid have in mind for calculating the area of the puddle?

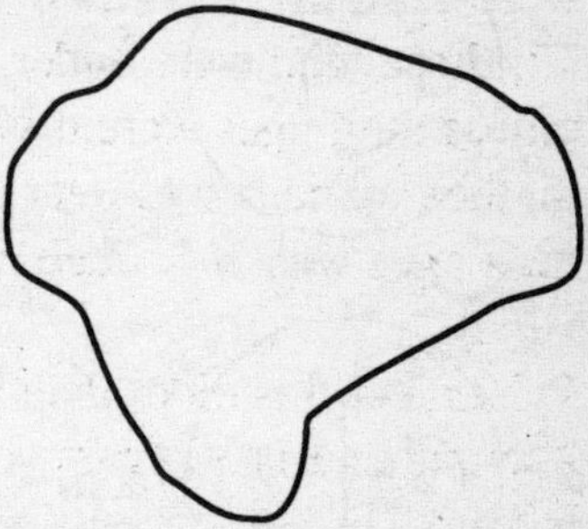

Q88 ★★★★ A40

Numbers

Four natives on an island were asked to explain their system of numbers.

Native 1 said: '18 is a prime number and so is 41.'
Native 2 said: '7 x 8 = 62.'
Native 3 said: '35 is a prime number.'
Native 4 said: '63 is evenly divisible by 4.'

Two of the natives were telling the truth; two of the natives were lying. What is the base of their system?

Analogy

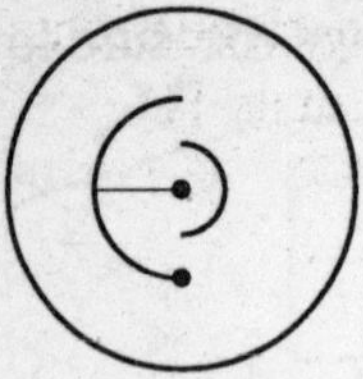

is to

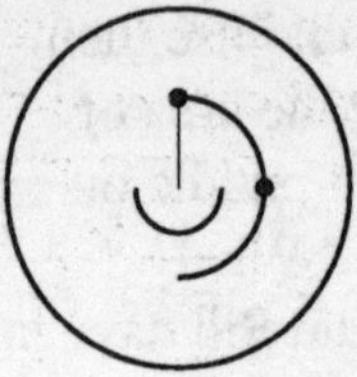

as

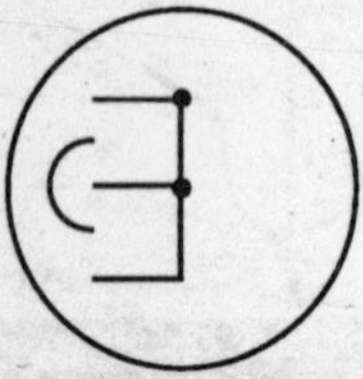

is to

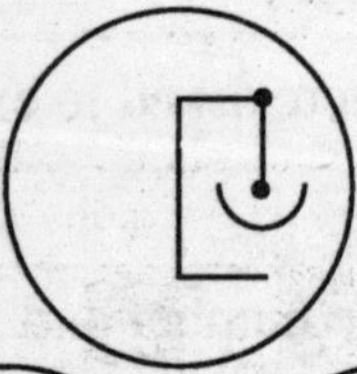

A

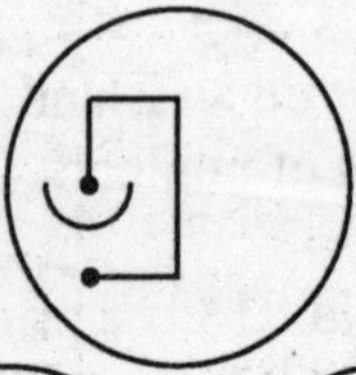

B

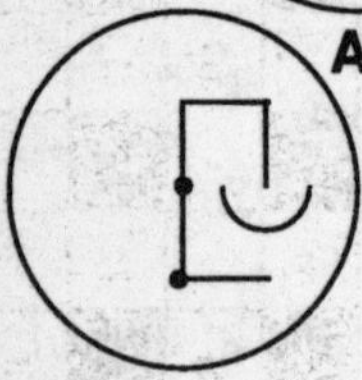

C

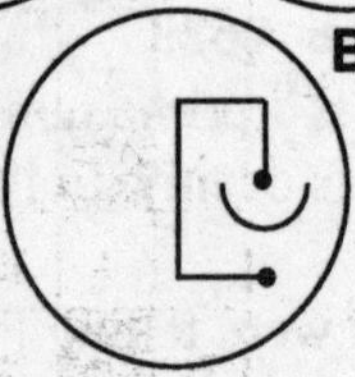

D

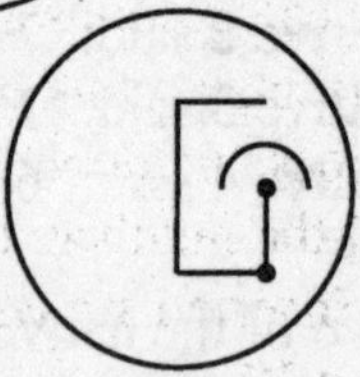

E

Q90 ★ ★ ★ A56

Square of the Sixth Order

Insert the remaining numbers from 1 to 36 to produce a magic square in which each horizontal, vertical and corner-to-corner line totals 111.

	35				
30					
		15			
				20	
		10			25
				5	

Q91 ★ ★ ★ A20

Brain Strain

Insert numbers into the remaining blank squares so that all the calculations are correct, reading both across and down. All the numbers to be inserted are less than 10.

	-		+		=	4
x	■	x	■	+	■	+
	+		-	3	=	
÷	■	÷	■	-	■	-
	÷	2	+		=	
=	■	=	■	=	■	=
9	-		+		=	

Q92 ★ ★ ★ ★ A84

Thirteenth-century Word Search

Definitions are given for 16 words, all of which date from the thirteenth to the seventeenth century. The words run in any direction in the grid but only in a straight line. Every letter is used, and some are used twice.

Y	T	N	I	A	D	E	M	K	C	I	R	P
R	F	E	L	L	O	W	F	E	E	L	R	E
R	L	E	U	S	E	L	F	R	U	M	E	R
O	E	N	B	S	P	R	U	W	Y	R	B	U
S	S	O	B						L	E	M	E
O	H	B	E						L	I	I	L
G	S	I	R						O	R	T	P
Y	P	L	W						L	C	Y	T
R	A	L	O						P	M	L	N
R	D	E	R	S	P	M	U	T	O	I	L	A
E	E	B	T	S	K	A	E	K	P	A	E	H
M	S	M	E	L	L	S	M	O	C	K	B	C
S	E	L	B	B	U	F	E	L	B	B	U	M

1. The person who cries aim at archery
2. A lovely maiden, a pretty lass
3. Food, provisions
4. To sing and weep at the same time
5. To crawl into the skin of another
6. Fingernails
7. Cackles
8. Food and drink that makes one idle (junk food)
9. A tale that evokes joy and sadness
10. Depression of the spirits
11. Freckles, pimples
12. A little darling or mistress
13. A fancy dresser
14. A licentious man
15. Glances of the eye
16. Places for storing ammunition, usually surrounded by high walls

CROSSWORD VARIATIONS

Crossword puzzles are probably the best known type of puzzle in existence, and they are attempted by an enormous number of people every day all over the globe and in all different languages. There are no conventional crosswords in this section, although each puzzle is a variation on the traditional crossword theme.

Nursery Rhyme Crossword 1

Hidden in the narrative are eight clues. Find them, solve them and enter the solutions in the grid.

Jack Sprat, who owned a Greek warship and was one of the excavators, could eat no fat.

His best loved wife, who was one of several young ladies and who was drugged, could eat no lean, and so between them they planned to lick the platter clean of Atlantic fish, from which she extracts essences.

Q94 ★ ★ ★ A104

Alphabet Crossword

Insert the 26 letters of the alphabet in the grid to complete the crossword. Seven letters have already been put in place, and one clue is given.

Clue: American drink of spirit and mint.

A B C D E F G ~~H~~ I ~~J~~ ~~K~~ L M

N O P ~~Q~~ R S T U V ~~W~~ ~~X~~ ~~Y~~ Z

Diamond Crossword

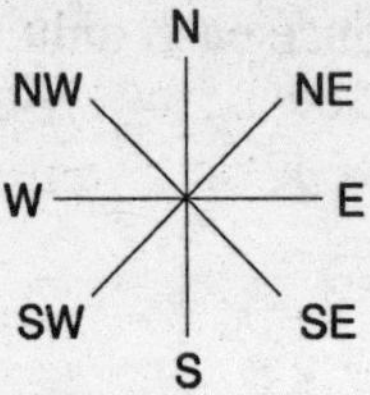

In this unusual crossword all the answers run in the direction of compass points. There are just enough clues to enable all 36 squares to be completed.

Clues:

1. NE Gloomy
1. SE Specimen
3. NE Of time, pass
5. NW Get free
3. N Landed property
1. E Type of light cake
6. W Pal
7. S Region
2. S Dull blow
4. W Rhythmic composition

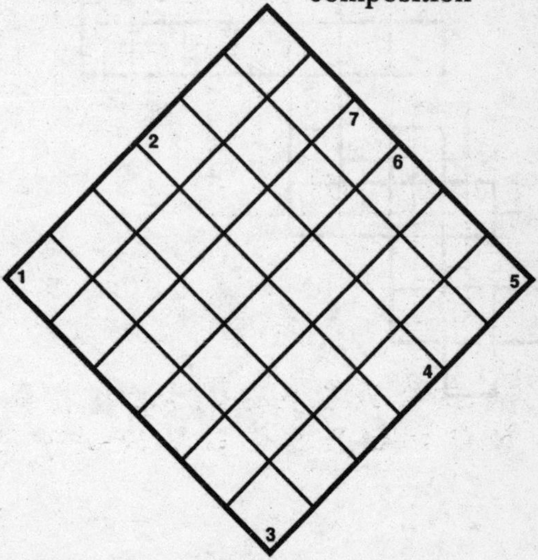

Cross-alphabet

Insert the 26 letters of the alphabet once each only to form a crossword.

Clues (in no particular order):

Invigorating excitement
Expeditiously
Undulating
Bovine mammal
Fear and trembling
Seed case
Stoop
A preserve

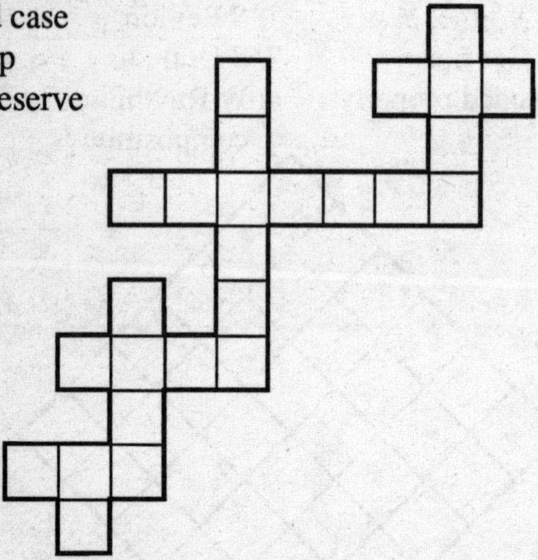

Q97 ★★ A60

Clueless Crossword

In each square are four letters. Your task is to cross out three of the four, leaving one letter in each square so that the crossword is made up of interlocking words in the usual way.

S T R P	I R A E	B Q R S	T A U R	P J A E	C K R D	A T E N
O R I U		E O R U		N E M A		A J M C
E T D R	E A W R	O I S A	S M U A	G B P E	A I T L	S E N T
A G N L		I S V T		O E L F		P C N E
L N E T	X N A M	E N T S	E R S A	D Y N E	E R A O	E T D N

Q98 ★ ★ A63

Target Crossword

Find 16 six-letter words by pairing up the 32 three-letter bits.

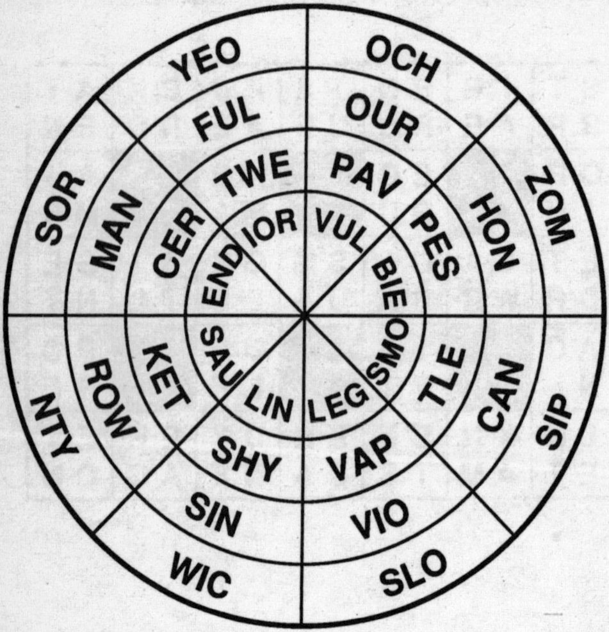

Q99 ★★ A41

Tiles

Place the tiles in the grid to complete the crossword.

OAS	OW	NE	E	~~R~~
AIS	AC	TT	S	K
~~DEC~~	~~IS~~	~~LE~~	C	R
ATE	IS	~~ER~~	R	E
OBI	ER		D	N
LIN	MO		T	E
TWI	NK		R	E
VAN	LE		A	R

Q100 ★ ★ ★ A19

Nursery Rhyme Crossword 2

Hidden in the narrative are eight clues. Find them, solve them and enter the solutions in the grid.

The owl and a certain type of armadillo went to sea in a precious stone colour green boat, which was used to lift up mud from the sea bed. They took with them some honey and some tough, white flexible tissue and plenty of small middle Eastern coins wrapped up in a five pound note. The armadillo became sorrowful because they could not find the sea-side places.

Q101 ★ ★ A54

Alphabet Crossword

Complete the crossword using all 26 letters of the alphabet once each only, apart from the letters that have already been inserted.

	■	O	■		R	O		
A	C	R		■		■		■
	■		■		U		R	E
O		I		■	G	■		■
R	■	T	I	G		T	■	
■	W	■	C	■	S		R	E
	A			S	■		■	
■		■	E	■	S	T	Y	E
		E	R		■	S	■	R

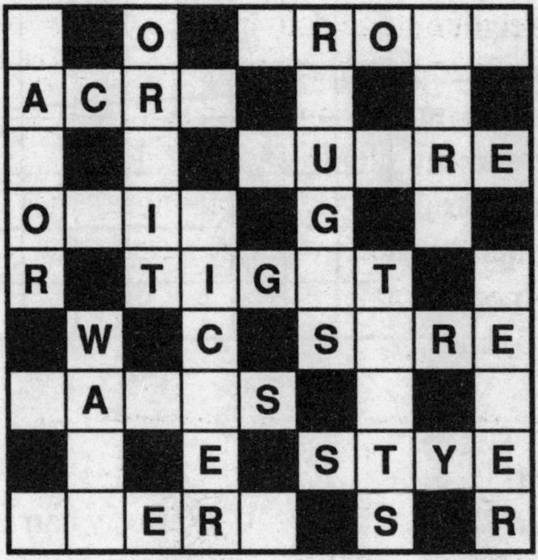

A B C D E F G H I J K L M
N O P Q R S T U V W X Y Z

Q102 ★★ A37

Directional Crossword

The answers run horizontally, vertically or diagonally, to either the right or the left. Each solution starts on the lower number and finishes on the next high number – i.e., 1 to 2, 2 to 3, and so on.

1	5							4
10			13			12		7
	17						15	
							14	
				16				
11			8			9		6
3								2

1. Keeper
2. Incubus
3. Turned to account
4. Cause anxiety
5. Echinoderm with five arms
6. Female entitled to legacy
7. Firmer
8. Fanatical
9. Disputes
10. Railway carriages storage places
11. Orange-yellow
12. Bird's home
13. Attempted
14. Fish
15. Fixes tightly
16. Flat thick stone
17. Marshy ground

Magic Word Square

Rearrange the 25 letters to form five different five-letter words, which, when placed correctly in the second grid, form a magic word square in which the five words read the same both across and down.

A	V	E	R	T
T	R	I	P	E
S	L	E	E	P
S	P	I	N	E
P	A	V	E	S

Pyramid Quotation

'Life is like a tennis game, you can't win without serving.'

Use all 45 letters of the above quotation to complete the pyramid with one one-letter, one two-letter, one three-letter, one four-letter, one five-letter, one six-letter, one seven-letter, one eight-letter and one nine-letter word. The clues are in no particular order.

Clues:

Soft and smooth
Artificial hair
Garden flower
Unrestrained and vicious
The pronoun of the first person singular
Sensible
Undecided
Musical composition
Belonging to me

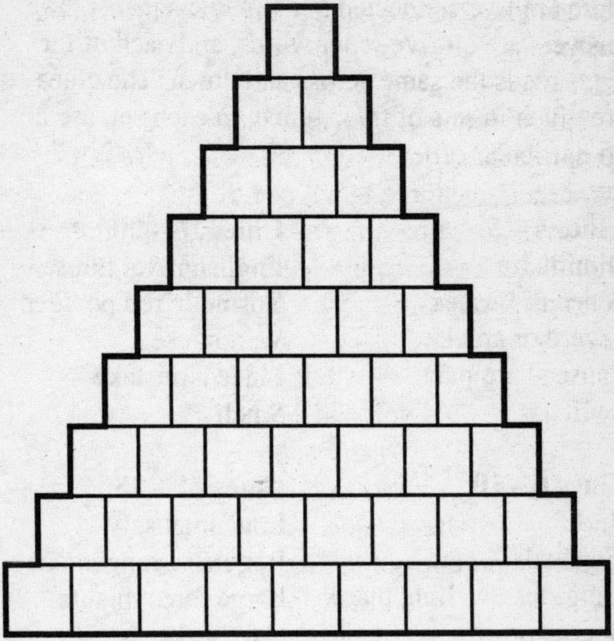

Magic Squares

Here are five connected 5 x 5 magic squares. The answers are all five-letter words, and each of the grids reads the same across and down. The clues are given in sets of five, which, in each set, are in no particular order.

Clues 1 – 5
Diminish
Fence of bushes
Severe or cruel
Cause sharp pain
Swift

Clues 6 – 10
Nude
Finished
Religious dwelling place
Once more
Sift and strain

Clues 11 – 15
Eastern person
Horseman's spear
Huge person
Come into
Bird of prey

Clues 16 – 20
English royal house
Cosmetic red powder
Warehouse
Made a mistake
Smell

Clues 21 – 25
Love intensely
Regular arrangement
Large forest plants
Oven bake
Work for

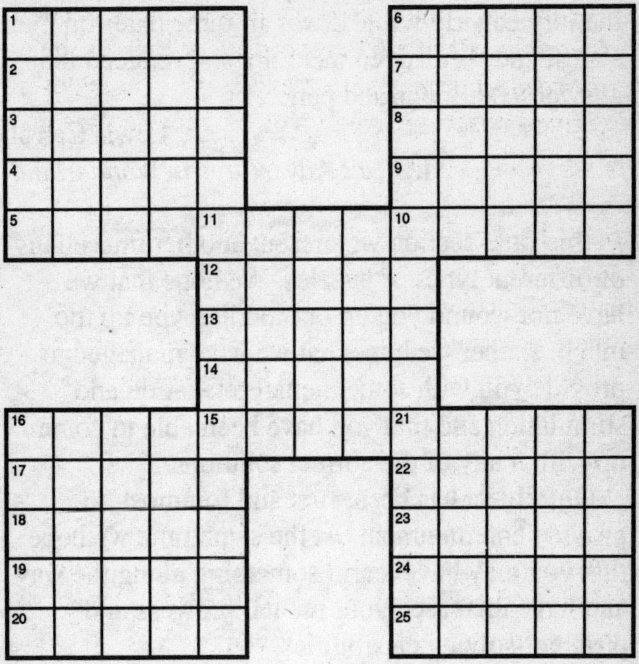
1
2
3
4
5
6
7
8
9
10
11
12
13
14
15
16
17
18
19
20
21
22
23
24
25

WIND-UPS

'Write that down,' the King said to the jury, and the jury eagerly wrote down all three dates on their slates, and then added them up, and reduced the answer to shillings and pence.'

Lewis Carroll
(*Alice's Adventures in Wonderland*)

In this final section we present another miscellany of different types of puzzles. We hope that we have not wound you up or muddled you up too much. Rather we hope that we have managed to provide you with some mental relaxation and stimulation and that you have been able to come up with many of the correct solutions.

Our object has been, first and foremost, to provide entertainment. At the same time we hope that you may have learnt something along the way and have increased your mental prowess and problem-solving capabilities.

Q106 ★ A49

Cryptogram

This appears to be one of those cryptograms in which each letter of the alphabet is substituted by another. Can you solve it?

M ISC HIEV OUSO FM
ETOT RYTOTR ICKY OU

Just for interest, the frequency table for letters of the English language is as follows:

ETAOINSRHLDCUMFPGWYBVKXJQZ

Q107 ★★ A24

The Eternal Mozart

My compact disc player has a shuffle facility whereby it plays the tracks on a compact disc in random order. Alternatively, if I wish I can program it so that the tracks can be played in any order I want. My favourite Mozart CD has 10 tracks. If I decided to play the disc once each day and program the 10 tracks to be played in a different order each day, how long would it take before I had heard the 10 tracks played in every possible different order?

Q108 ★★ A39

Cannon Ball

A cannon ball is fired from a cannon and travels for ¾ mile horizontally before falling to earth. At the same time as the first cannon ball is fired, a second cannon ball is dropped vertically at the same height as the mouth of the cannon.

Which cannon ball hits the ground first?

Q109 ★★★ A67

The Journey

My pleasant journey commences when I briefly meet a familiar character in front of a wooden strip. I then pass several apartments with many whimsical fancies among a fine array of glossary. Often feeling a tremble, I find many keen edges between several siestas. My journey ends when I reach a place of refreshment. Where has my journey taken me?

Q110 ★★ A57

Nine Trees

'Take nine conifers from the nursery,' said the head gardener to his assistant, 'and plant them so that there are 10 straight rows with three trees in each row.' 'I think that's impossible,' said the assistant. 'Not at all,' said the head gardener, 'there is a perfectly symmetric way in which it can be done, but I'll let you work it out for yourself.'

How did the gardener's assistant carry out the task he had been set?

Q111 ★★★ A64

Drinks

Each horizontal line and each vertical line contains the jumbled letters of a type of drink, alcoholic or otherwise. Find the 20 drinks. Every letter in the grid is used once only.

G	U	U	R	U	R	D	R	M	E
I	C	T	M	K	G	L	N	Q	P
E	O	F	C	C	E	Y	C	A	F
A	C	D	C	R	E	I	B	E	J
E	T	T	A	P	A	A	E	U	L
O	O	P	O	T	S	R	Y	H	U
R	M	S	A	N	N	I	A	T	I
L	A	G	I	H	N	H	N	S	I
R	E	O	D	M	U	N	A	S	D
Y	O	S	L	R	H	S	D	E	R

Crazy Columns

Insert the four missing letters in the grid below.

A	G	H	E
I	N	C	O
C	B	P	C
P		O	B
M	L	O	C
	L	P	E
L	D	O	O
T	P	I	E
S		A	E
M	D	H	O
E	O	U	I
S	A		K

Q113 ★ A48

Palindromic Years

1991 was a palindromic year as will be the year 2002, a gap of 11 years. When was the last time there was a shorter gap betwen two palindromic years and when will be the next time?

Q114 ★ A38

Frankenstein's Creation

For his latest creation Frankenstein takes a large portion from Trudy, a piece from Hermione, a slice from the middle of Brenda and a small part from Peggy. After he has put them all together, what does Frankenstein call his new creation?

Q115	★★★	A23

What the Dickens!

By starting somewhere in the letter-maze and by moving one letter at a time to the left or right, or up or down it is possible to spell out the titles of 10 works by Charles Dickens. It does not matter which title you identify first; provided you make the correct turnings, the titles will eventually lead you through the whole pattern of 144 letters.

B	E	Y	A	N	H	O	S	N	I	C	K
M	O	D	S	D	C	L	A	H	T	Y	L
I	S	T	O	N	I	Z	Z	E	O	B	E
W	T	R	N	T	E	L	U	D	L	I	O
O	L	E	H	I	W	C	H	C	U	R	S
S	I	V	A	R	I	N	H	S	Y	T	I
E	I	T	I	D	T	R	O	P	V	I	D
O	F	O	C	T	I	A	M	D	A	O	C
E	T	W	X	E	M	E	S	N	R	P	P
L	A	T	P	T	A	G	D	A	A	R	E
N	S	A	E	C	E	E	U	B	B	F	I
O	I	T	A	T	R	G	R	Y	D	L	E

ANSWERS

A1 Anagrams Introduction

The Washington Post

A2 Spherical Q78

Pious (sanctimonious); happiness (contentment); exodus (evacuation); riotous (disorderly); impetus (stimulus); confess (divulge); antics (tomfoolery); logistics (coordination)

A3 Nine-letter Words Q11

Limousine – the others contain numbers: teleph(one), fr(eight)er and drif(two)od.

A4 Diamond Crossword Q95

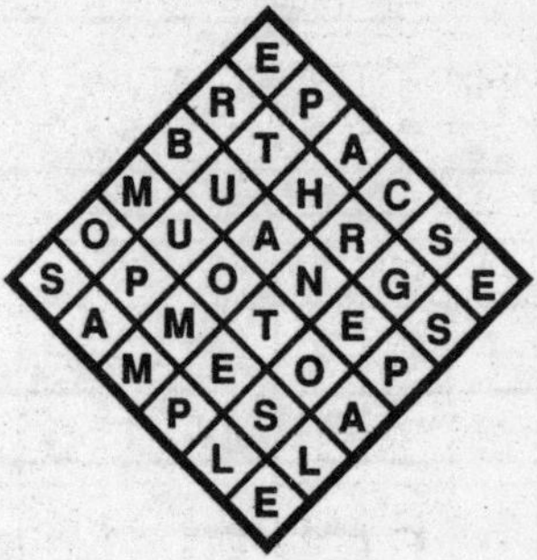

A5 Factorial Q86

5913=1!+2!+3!+4!+5!+6!+7!

A6 Crazy Columns Q112

Y, P, G and D – the word hippopotamus can be read downwards, alternating between columns 3 and 1; the word accomplished appears in columns 1 and 3; the word encyclopedia in columns 4 and 2; and gobbledegook in columns 2 and 4.

A7 Sequence Q49

B – each of the five circles containing a pattern moves in its own individual sequence – e.g., the black circle moves two forward, three back, two forward; the circle with the cross moves two back, two forward, two back and so on.

A8 Lewis Q41

Lewis is Lewis Carroll; ML8ML8 sounds like 'I'm late, I'm late' – (the words of the White Rabbit in *Alice's Adventures in Wonderland*). The Rabbit is a Volkswagen car.

A9 Keywords Q2

1. Mistaken; 2. Cabbage; 3. Important

A10 Odd One Out Q15

E – A is the same as F; B is the same as C; D is the same as G.

A11 The Magic 11 Q37

1	4	2	8	5	7
4	2	8	5	7	1
2	8	5	7	1	4
8	5	7	1	4	2
5	7	1	4	2	8
7	1	4	2	8	5

A12	No-repeat Letters	Q29

Trampoline

A13	Riddle	Q6

Plant

A14	Five Words	Q57

They begin with the word five in different languages – Go (Japanese), Fünf (German), Fem (Danish), Pende (Greek) and Bes (Turkish)

A15	Advance Matrix	Q52

C – the outlines in the first column are added to those in the second column. However, lines and the dot disappear where they correspond so that lines and a dot appear in the third column only when they are different.

A16	Anagram Theme	Q80

1. Radish (is hard); parsnip (rip snap); spinach (chin sap); turnip (pit run); shallot (to halls); broccoli (cool crib); lettuce (tee cult)
2. Dublin (lid bun); Santiago (stain ago); Athens (has ten); Belgrade (glad beer); Canberra (race barn); Prague (rug ape); Madrid (add rim)

A17	Missing Number	Q72

2 – the numbers in the first two horizontal and vertical lines, divided by either 5 or 4, give the figure in the final column or row. For example, 15÷5=3, 8÷4=2, 3+2=5.

A18 Magic Square Q64

23	6	19	2	15
10	18	1	14	22
17	5	13	21	9
4	12	25	8	16
11	24	7	20	3

A19 Nursery Rhyme Question 2 Q100

D	R	E	D	G	E	R
A		M		R		E
S	P	E	C	I	E	S
Y		R		S		O
P	I	A	S	T	E	R
U		L		L		T
S	A	D	D	E	N	S

A20 Brain Strain Q91

8	-	7	+	3	=	4
x		x		+		+
9	+	2	-	3	=	8
÷		÷		-		-
8	÷	2	+	2	=	6
=		=		=		=
9	-	7	+	4	=	6

A21 The Knight's Tour Q3

More people are coming to realize how much fun there can be in the solving of simple little maths teasers.

A22 Letters and Numerals Q14

Replace each number with the appropriate Roman numeral and you will obtain the words Lynx, Cedar, Eland, Camel, Llama and Bull. Cedar is the odd one out because the others are animals.

A23 What the Dickens Q115

Martin Chuzzlewit, Nicholas Nickleby, The Old Curiosity Shop, David Copperfield, Barnaby Rudge, Great Expectations, A Tale of Two Cities, Oliver Twist, Dombey and Son, Hard Times

A24 The Eternal Mozart Q107

10x9x8x7x6x5x4x3x2x1=3628800 days or 9941 years (excluding leap years)

A25 Four Teasers Q4

1. 8lb
2. Because if number nine had been working the chief engineer would have said 'seven out of eight are not working'.
3. 157 – 1728 ends give 144 cigarettes; 144 ends give 12 cigarettes; 12 ends give one further cigarette – giving a total of 157.
4. Z – D+3 = H+4 = M+5 = S+6 = Z

A26 Odd One Out Introduction

The triangle containing the letter A is the odd one out. In all the others the number of sides of the figure coincides with the position in the alphabet of the letter within it.

A27 Kickself Introduction

Lewis Carroll made sure that the number he wrote added to the number above it totalled 9999. The answer was therefore bound to be 3144+9999+9999=23142

A28 Square Q26

Laughable

H	L	U	B	A	E
E	L	A	G	G	A
B	B	U	L	L	A
A	A	A	U	H	L
U	L	G	A	E	B
H	L	G	E	H	L

A29 Seven Clues Q59

The Seven Dwarfs – Sneezy, Doc, Grumpy, Happy, Sleepy, Bashful and Dopey

A30 Jigsaw Puzzle Q51

3 – square, rectangle and Greek cross

A31 Analogy Q45

B – the sides of the first figure are parallel with those in the second figure.

A32 Anagrams Introduction

Take Indian child, explore West

A33 Square Numbers Q67

The lowest square number is 139854276; the highest is 923187456.

A34 Letter Sequences Q1

1. F – they are the first letters of the words first, second, third, fourth and fifth.
2. A – the letters are extracted from the days of the week in the following sequence: S is the first letter of the first day (Sunday), O is the second letter of the second day (Monday) and so on. A is the seventh letter of the seventh day (Saturday).
3. Z – they are initial letters of the Greek alphabet – alpha, beta, gamma, delta, epsilon and zeta
4. F – they are the first letter of the second names of US presidents in reverse order – Clinton, Bush, Reagan, Reagan, Carter, Ford.
5. J – they are initials of the months arranged first according to the number of days, then in alphabetical order when the number of days is equal. The next month in the list is therefore July.

A35 Nonsense Sentences Q13

3 – in the others each word is an anagram of a capital city – Rome, Oslo, Lagos; Malé, Manila, Paris; La Paz, Lima, Seoul.

A36 Anagrammed Quotation Q81

The words go into the passage in the following order – moments (2), eternal (8), silence (6), perish (7), neither (4), listlessness (5), endeavour (10), emnity (1), abolish (3), destroy (9).

A37 Directional Crossword Q102

1. Custodian, 2. Nightmare, 3. Exploited, 4. Distress, 5. Starfish, 6. Heiress, 7. Stiffer, 8. Rabid, 9. Differs, 10. Sidings, 11. Saffron, 12. Nest, 13. Tried, 14. Dab, 15. Beds, 16. Slab, 17. Bog

[1] C	[5] S	S	E	R	T	S	I	[4] D
[10] S	U	T	[13] T	S	E	[12] N	E	[7] S
I	R	S	A	R	O	T	T	S
D	[17] B	E	T	R	I	I	[15] B	E
I	O	A	F	O	F	E	A	R
N	G	F	L	F	D	I	[14] D	I
G	A	P	E	[16] S	I	I	S	E
[11] S	X	R	[8] A	B	I	[9] D	A	[6] H
[3] E	R	A	M	T	H	G	I	[2] N

A38 Frankenstein's Creation Q114

Ermentrude – Hermoine, Brenda, Trudy, Peggy

A39 Cannon Ball Q108

Both cannon balls hit the ground at the same time.

A40 Numbers Q88

The base is 9. Natives 1 and 2 told the truth; natives 3 and 4 told lies.

A41 Tiles Q99

D	E	C	L	I	N	A	T	E
E		R		C		S		A
O	B	I		O	A	S	I	S
D		M	O	N	K			T
O	W	E	R		I	S	L	E
R			A	C	N	E		R
A	I	S	L	E		V	A	N
N		K		R		E		E
T	W	I	T	T	E	R	E	R

A42 Logic Q7

Q – the position in the alphabet of the letter in the middle is the average of the positions in the alphabet of the four letters surrounding it.

A43 The Hidden Message Q19

Take the fifth word, then count six and take the next word, then count seven and take the next word and so on to reveal the message 'The supplies will arrive early Tuesday morning'.

A44	Equation	Q35

$7^2=49$ – the 6 has been turned over to turn it into a 9.

A45	Word Construction	Q30

Barbecue, infantry, fatherland, discourage, artifice, outwardbound, soupkitchen, pollinate, meadowland, beleaguered

A46	Reverse Anagram	Q73

Hydraulics

A47	Connections	Q70

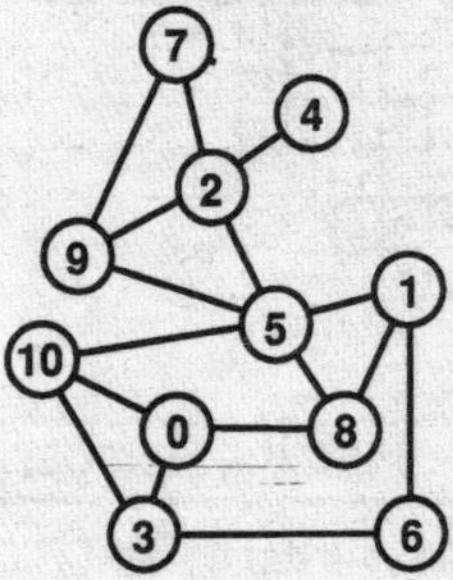

A48	Palindromic Years	Q113

The last time was between the years 999 and 1001, a gap of just two years. The next occasion will be in approximately 8000 years, in the years 9999 and 10001.

A49	Cryptogram	Q106

Mischievous of me to try to trick you (sorry about that!)

A50 An Ancient Fraction Q82

The fraction produces a number that is a fairly accurate approximation of pi – it is within 1.0000000848 of its value. Another way of arriving at the same figure – 3.1415929 – is by using the integers 3, 7 and 16. Take the reciprocal of 16 (i.e., 1÷16 = 0.0625) and add 7=7.0625. Take the reciprocal of this number (i.e., 1÷7.0625 = 0.1415929) and add 3 = 3.1415929.

A51 Cross-alphabet Q96

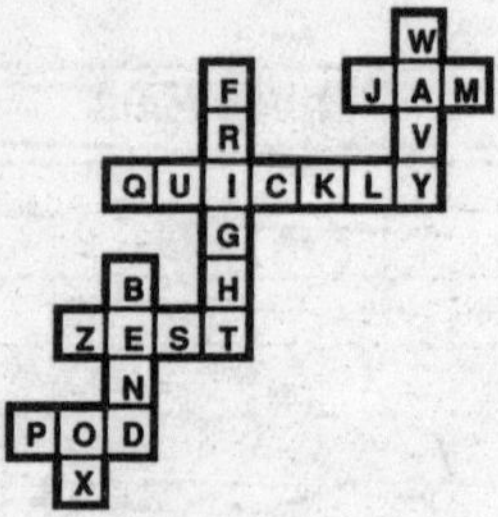

A52 Find the Number Q8

Two thousand nine hundred and forty – MMCMXL

A53 Three-letter Words Q18

Take the first letter of the first word, the second letter of the second word, the third letter of the third word, then the first letter of the fourth word and so on to reveal the message 'more power to your elbow'.

A54 Alphabet Crossword Q101

R		O		G	R	O	W	L
A	C	R	E		O		A	
Z		B		Q	U	I	R	E
O	M	I	T		G		P	
R		T	I	G	H	T		N
	W		C		S	U	R	E
J	A	C	K	S		F		V
	X		E		S	T	Y	E
D	Y	E	R	S		S		R

A55 A Magic '260' Q83

1	63	62	61	4	59	2	8
56	10	54	53	52	11	15	9
24	47	19	44	45	22	42	17
25	34	35	28	29	38	39	32
40	31	30	36	37	27	26	33
41	18	43	21	20	46	23	48
16	50	14	12	13	51	55	49
57	7	3	5	60	6	58	64

A56 Square of the Sixth Order Q90

1	35	4	33	32	6
30	8	27	28	11	7
24	23	15	16	14	19
13	17	21	22	20	18
12	26	10	9	29	25
31	2	34	3	5	36

A57 Nine Trees Q110

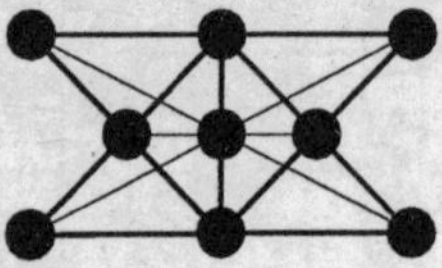

A58 Magic Squares Q105

H	A	R	S	H				M	A	N	S	E
A	B	A	T	E				A	G	A	I	N
R	A	P	I	D				N	A	K	E	D
S	T	I	N	G				S	I	E	V	E
H	E	D	G	E	A	G	L	E	N	D	E	D
				A	S	I	A	N				
				G	I	A	N	T				
				L	A	N	C	E				
S	T	O	R	E	N	T	E	R	O	A	S	T
T	U	D	O	R				O	R	D	E	R
O	D	O	U	R				A	D	O	R	E
R	O	U	G	E				S	E	R	V	E
E	R	R	E	D				T	R	E	E	S

A59 Find the Lady Q10

Deidre – all the other names appear in US States: Indiana, Maryland and Carolina.

A60 Clueless Crossword Q97

T	E	R	R	A	C	E
I		O		M		J
T	R	O	U	B	L	E
L		S		L		C
E	N	T	R	E	A	T

A61 Stair-rods Q87

Lay the stair-rods across the puddle, making sure that they are equal distances apart, measure the length of each stair-rod from top to bottom of the puddle as indicated by the arrows and add the measurements together. Divide the figure so obtained by the number of stair-rods lying across the puddle, and then multiply that figure by the width of the puddle to give the area.

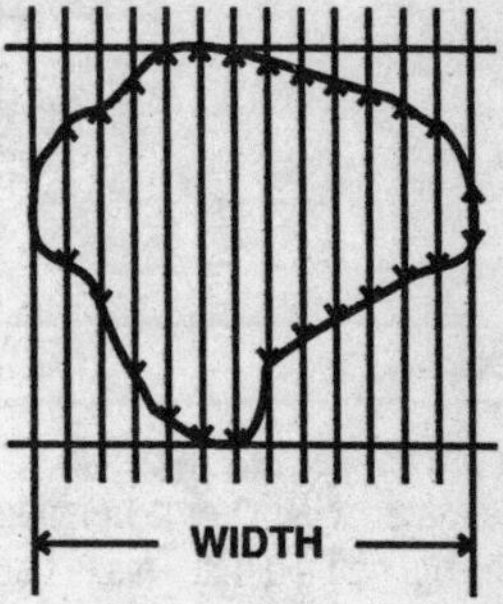

A62 Odd One Out Q12

C – the others, cut in half vertically, all form words – i.e., elf, cell and fleece – as do their mirror images.

A63 Target Crossword Q98

Vulcan, wicket, yeoman, zombie, violin, vapour, twenty, legend, sorrow, sloshy, smooch, sinful, siphon, saucer, pavior, pestle

A64 Drinks Q111

The letters in across words are circled.

G	Ⓤ	U	R	U	Ⓡ	D	R	Ⓜ	E	RUM
Ⓘ	C	T	Ⓜ	Ⓚ	G	Ⓛ	N	Q	P	MILK
Ⓔ	Ⓞ	Ⓕ	C	C	Ⓔ	Y	Ⓒ	A	Ⓕ	COFFEE
A	C	Ⓓ	Ⓒ	Ⓡ	E	Ⓘ	B	Ⓔ	J	CIDER
E	Ⓣ	T	A	P	Ⓐ	A	Ⓔ	U	L	TEA
Ⓞ	O	Ⓟ	O	Ⓣ	S	Ⓡ	Y	H	U	PORT
Ⓡ	Ⓜ	S	Ⓐ	N	Ⓝ	Ⓘ	A	Ⓣ	Ⓘ	MARTINI
L	A	Ⓖ	I	H	N	H	Ⓝ	S	Ⓘ	GIN
R	Ⓔ	O	D	Ⓜ	U	N	Ⓐ	S	Ⓓ	MEAD
Ⓨ	O	Ⓢ	L	Ⓡ	Ⓗ	S	D	Ⓔ	Ⓡ	SHERRY
LAGER	COCOA	STOUT	CORDIAL	PUNCH	NEGUS	SHANDY	BRANDY	SQUASH	JULEP	

A65 Game Show Q84

This puzzle was featured in the *Mail on Sunday*, but was not fully investigated. Half the mathematicians who were consulted favoured changing, half did not. This is because there are two possible answers. If the host did not know what was behind each door, then there would be no merit in changing. If, however, the host did know what was behind each door, you should change because your chances double.

A66 Analogy Q89

D

A67 The Journey Q109

Through a piece of music – character = clef; wooden strips = stave; several apartments = flats; whimsical fancies = crochets; array of glossary = notes; tremble = quaver; keen edges = sharps; siestas = rests; public house = bar

A68 The Caesar Alphabet Q17

'All bad precedents began as justifiable measures' (which is attributed to Julius Caesar himself).

A69 Peoples Q55

Belgian and Bengali are anagrams.

A70 Number Sequence Q43

1. 111 – these are numbers that, when written, appear the same when viewed upside down.
2. 55 – these are numbers that appear the same when viewed upside down on a calculator.

A71 What's the Connection Q61

Each has an anagram partner on the same theme – lemon (fruit); Kyoto (Japanese city); Arnold (man's name).

A72 Letter Sequences Q42

1. AE – these are the alternate letters from England, Ireland, Scotland and Wales.
2. UY – these are the alternate letters from the months of the year.

A73 Anagrammed Synonyms Q79

1. Grit – fortitude; 2. Dive – plummet; 3. Heart – interior; 4. Die – perish; 5. Mood – disposition; 6. Plain – Apparent; 7. Clip – curtail; 8. Prone – prostrate; 9. Team – troupe; 10. Mate – comrade; 11. Top – pinnacle; 12. Old – ancient; 13. Note – message; 14. Urge – entreat; 15. Lone – deserted

This is a simple mathematical problem. There are five variables, each of which affects the day of the week upon which any date falls, and by substituting numbers for those variables we can find the day of the week for any date over a period of 200 years. The variables are as follows.

Century – an adjustment is needed at each change of century: 1900+ is fixed at 0, 2000+ will require an adjustment of – 1. This adjustment covers the first two digits of the year.

Year – we now need to look at the last two digits of the year. Because there are 365 days in the year, which when divided by 7 leaves a remainder of 1, the same date each year will be advanced by one day – for example 5 January 1922 was a Thursday, 5 January 1923 was a Friday – we therefore take the last two figures as actual – i.e., 99.

Leap year – this occurs every four years, and the jump is therefore two days instead of one day for each year that passes. This is covered by adding ¼ of the last two digits of the year and ignoring any remainder – i.e., 99x¼=24.

Day – use the actual day – i.e., 31.

Month – a code is shown for the month as follows, Jan=1, Jan LP=0, Feb=4, Feb LP=3, Mar=4, Apr=0, May=2, Jun=5, Jul=0, Aug=3, Sep=6, Oct=1, Nov=4, Dec=6. Because the effect of a leap year is not felt until 29 February, a different code number is used for January and February during leap years.

Our calculation is therefore as follows for 31 December 1999.

Century 19=0
Last two digits of year=99
Leap years @ ¼=24
Day=31
Month Dec=6
Total =160, divided by 7 gives a remainder of 6
Key: Sun=1, Mon=2, Tue=3, Wed=4, Thur=5, Fri=6, Sat=0
Answer FRIDAY

A75 Letter Change Q9

1. Just the job; 2. Fun and games; 3. In full cry; 4. Go like a dream; 5. Run rings around; 6. Tooth and nail; 7. Blow hot and cold; 8. Play on words; 9. Hide and seek; 10. Play with fire; 11. Take in good part; 12. Turn a deaf ear; 13. Name the day; 14. Old wives tale; 15. With open arms; 16. In the raw; 17. Out of order; 18. Live and let live; 19. Get a move on; 20. Any old how

A76 The Polybius Cipher Q16

Read the numbers down and across to find the number in each letter – e.g., H=23. 'The world's great men have not commonly been great scholars, nor its great scholars great men.'

Oliver Wendell Holmes

	1	2	3	4	5
1	A	B	C	D	E
2	F	G	H	IJ	K
3	L	M	N	O	P
4	Q	R	S	T	U
5	V	W	X	Y	Z

A77 Square Words Q27

Necessary – requisite; calculate – determine; luxuriant – excessive

A78 Discs Q53

B – each section moves in its own individual sequence. The dots move three places anticlockwise; the solid sections move two places clockwise; the cross-hatched sections move one place clockwise; the lined sections move three places anticlockwise; and the white sections move two places clockwise, then two places anticlockwise.

A79 Logic Q46

B – first one half of the figure flips round, then the next, and becomes attached to the first available surface of its other half.

A80 Peaks Q44

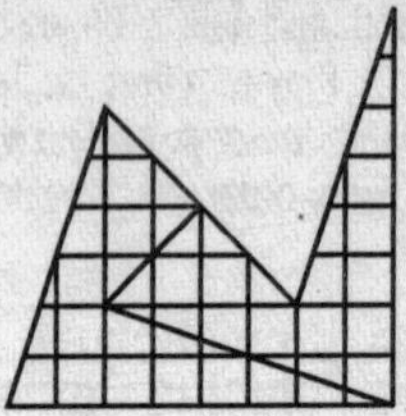

A81 Anagrammed Phrases Q74

1. A foot in both camps; 2. Serves you right; 3. To bring to bear; 4. Like grim death; 5. Tom Dick and Harry.

A82 Magic Square Q71

24	8	17	1	15
16	5	14	23	7
13	22	6	20	4
10	19	3	12	21
2	11	25	9	18

A83 Numbers Introduction

8	1	6
3	5	7
4	9	2

A84 Thirteenth-Century Word Search Q92

1. Aimcrier, 2. Bellibone, 3. Bellytimber, 4. Chantpleure, 5. Fellowfeel, 6. Flesh-spades, 7. Keaks, 8. Lubberwort, 9. Merry-go-sorry, 10. Mubbles-fubbles, 11. Murfles, 12. Poplolly, 13. Prick-me-dainty, 14. Smellsmock, 15. Wurps, 16. Tumps

A85 Mathematicians Q85

Their ages were: 1 – 38; 2 – 39; 3 – 68; 4 – 29; 5 – 26; 6 – 61

A86 Cryptokey 1 Q22

'Time flies; I can't, they come past at such irregular intervals' Keyed phrase: Tempus Fugit (TEMPUSFGI)

A87 Work It Out Q39

Making a mountain out of a molehill

A88 Categorize Q32

European currency (punt, pound, mark); boats (smack, barge, tramp); walk (slog, trek, hike); batter (hammer, beat, thrash)

A89 Words Q54

Taking A=1, B=2, C=3 and so on, the sum of the letters in each word totals 100, as do the letters in Socrates and Robin Hood.

A90 Words Q75

The 14-letter words are: 1. Administration, 2. Extinguishable, 3. Correspondence, 4. Misappropriate, 5. Predeterminate. The 15-letter words are: 1. Cinematographer, 2. Psychotherapist, 3. Experimentation, 4. Comprehensively, 5. Totalitarianism

A91 Cryptosymbol Q20

This is a straight substitution cryptogram in which each letter of the alphabet is represented by a different symbol. Decoded, the quotation reads: 'Mr. Harris, plutocrat wants to give my cheek a pat, if the Harris pat means a Paris Hat, hooray!' Cole Porter

A92 Nursery Rhyme Crossword 1 Q93

S	E	D	A	T	E	D
C	■	A	■	R	■	I
H	E	R	R	I	N	G
E	■	L	■	R	■	E
M	A	I	D	E	N	S
E	■	N	■	M	■	T
D	I	G	G	E	R	S

A93 I'll Make a Wise Phrase Q77

1. King Lear, 2. Troilus and Cressida, 3. Much Ado About Nothing, 4. Loves Labours Lost, 5. The Comedy of Errors, 6. The Winter's Tale, 7. Coriolanus, 8. Romeo and Juliet, 9. Timon of Athens, 10. Titus Andronicus

A94 Magic Word Square Q103

P	A	P	E	R
A	L	I	V	E
P	I	P	E	S
E	V	E	N	T
R	E	S	T	S

A95 Cryptokey 2 Q23

'These two great organisations of the English speaking democracies, the British Empire and the United States, will have to be somewhat mixed up together in some of their affairs... I do not view the process with any misgivings. I could not stop it if I wished; no one can stop it. Like the Mississippi, it just keeps rolling along. Let it roll. Let it roll on in full flood, inexorable, irresistible, benignant, to broader lands and better days.' *Winston Churchill*

Keyed phrase: Hands across the sea (HANDSCROTE)

A96 Word Search Q33

The positive word form as in the grid is given first; the better known, negative form is given in brackets.
1. Advertent (inadvertent); 2. Infectant (disinfectant); 3. Histamine (antihistamine); 4. Corrigible (incorrigible); 5. Evitable (inevitable); 6. Odorant (deodorant); 7. Consolate (disconsolate); 8. Wieldy (unwieldy); 9. Canny (uncanny); 10. Biotic (antibiotic); 11. Couth (uncouth); 12. Effable (ineffable); 13. Kempt (unkempt); 14. Licit (illicit); 15. Furl (unfurl)

A97 Rebuses Q40

1. In a spot; 2. A square meal; 3. Sitting tenant; 4. Man about town; 5. Breaking loose; 6. Short measure; 7. Disorderly conduct; 8. Split pea; 9. A piece of the action; 10. Royal prerogative; 11. To read between the lines; 12. Index linked; 13. Part and parcel; 14. Long odds; 15. Mixed metaphor; 16. Industrial action; 17. No man is an island; 18. Mixed doubles; 19. Garden centre; 20. Backward glance; 21. The ends of the earth

A98 Dots Q50

E – the number dots of increases by one each time, and the dots are added horizontally, vertically downwards, horizontally and, finally, vertically downwards.

A99 Missing Square Q47

G – it is a magic square in which each horizontal, vertical and corner-to-corner line totals 15 and each number, from 1 to 9, is represented. Black circles are worth 2, and white circles are worth 1.

A100 Synchronized Synonyms Q24

Crack (fracture, splinter); Contemplate (meditate, ruminate); August (imposing, majestic); Subterfuge (artifice, pretence); Foreword (preamble, prologue); Childish (juvenile, immature); Viable (feasible, workable); Macabre (dreadful, ghoulish)

A101 Common Clues Q56

They all begin with white: white horses; white dwarf; white ensign; white elephant; white heat; white ant; white knight; white whale; white lie; white paper

A102 Athletes Q66

6 events scored at 6 points for first, 3 for second and 2 for third.

A103 Anagrams Q76

1. Caveat emptor; 2. counter clockwise; 3. ctenoid (an anagram of NOTICED; it means with a comb-shaped edge)

A104 Alphabet Crossword Q94

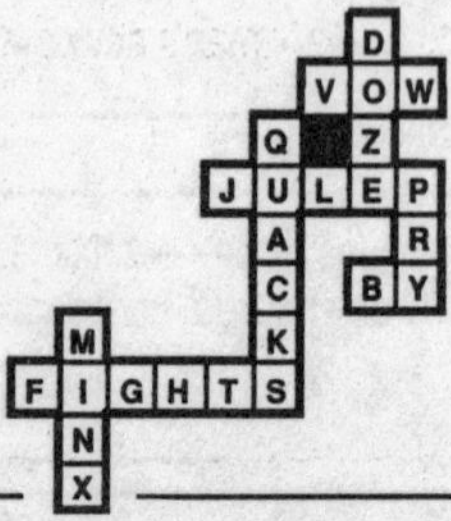

A105 Pyramid Quotation Q104

carnation, hesitant, violent, silken, fugue, wise, wig, my, I

A106 One Hundred Q68

$96 + \frac{2148}{537}$; $96 + \frac{1752}{438}$; $96 + \frac{1428}{357}$; $94 + \frac{1578}{263}$; $91 + \frac{7524}{836}$;

$91 + \frac{5742}{638}$; $82 + \frac{3546}{197}$; $81 + \frac{7524}{396}$; $81 + \frac{5643}{297}$; $3 + \frac{69258}{714}$

A107 What's the Link Q62

They are all books of the Bible – 1. Exodus; 2. Numbers; 3. Judges; 4. Ruth; 5. Kings; 6. Chronicles; 7. Job; 8. Proverbs; 9. Mark; 10. Revelation

A108 Pyramids Q31

1. Anaesthetically; 2. Superficialness

A109 Three Cryptograms Q21

1. 'I'm very well acquainted too with matters mathematical, I understand equations, both the simple and quadratical.' *W.S. Gilbert*

2. 'I remember being handed a score composed by Mozart at the age of eleven. What could I say? I felt like De Kooning who was asked to comment on a certain abstract painting and answered in the negative. He was then told it was the work of a celebrated monkey. "That's different. For a monkey it's terrific".' *Igor Stravinsky*

3. 'He who builds according to every man's advice will have a crooked house.' *Danish Proverb*

A110 Calculation Q38

9825 – turn the page upside down and add up the two numbers.

A111 Famous Names Q58

They are all capital cities of States of the United States.

A112 Symbols Q48

1.

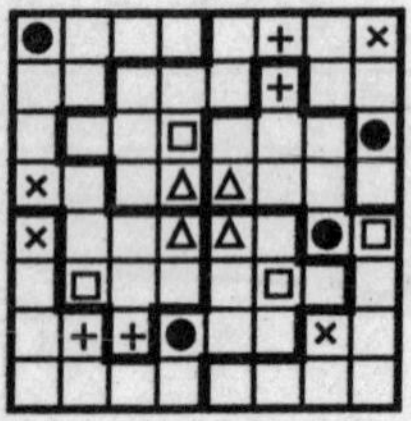

2.

A113 Strike Out Q36

A ~~T~~ S ~~E~~ H ~~N~~ ~~L~~ O ~~F~~ R T P ~~T~~ H ~~T~~ R ~~E~~ A ~~P~~ S E ~~S~~

A114 Hexagon Q34

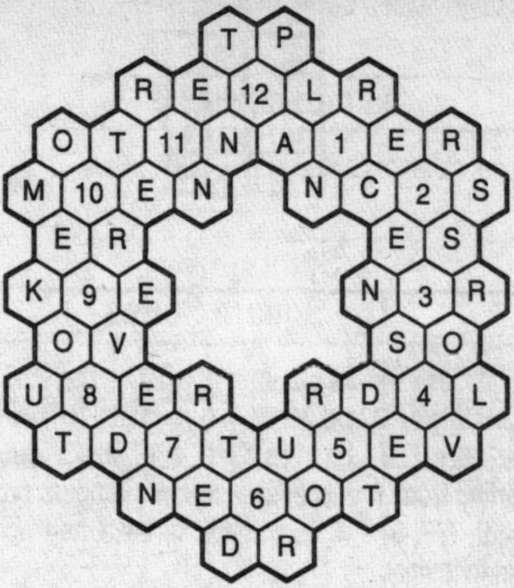

A115 Jumble Q25

Alternative, anticyclone, approximate, allegorical, archaically, arraignment, approbation, acupuncture

A116 Pyramid Word Q28

L, in, met, rust, saint – instrumentalist

A117 Who's Who Q60

They all bear people's names, either factual or fictional – 1. Mickey Finn; 2. Walter Mitty; 3. Hobson's choice; 4. Sally Lunn; 5. Davy Jones's locker; 6. Beau Brummell; 7. Sam Browne; 8. Tony; 9. Molotov cocktail; 10. Darby and Joan

A118 Numbers Introduction

10	4	13	7
15	5	12	2
8	14	3	9
1	11	6	16

A119 The Square Series Q65

Take, for example, the square number 784 (28^2). The sum of its digits is 19, which in turn totals 10 and which in turn totals 1. The next square number is 841 (29^2). The sum of its digits is 13, and the sum of these digits is 4. Starting from 1, successive square numbers produce the sequence 1, 4, 9, 7, 7, 9, 4, 1, 9, and this series, when worked out this way, will repeat to infinity.

A120 Shortbread and Shooting Stars Q63

They are all misnomers – 1. Dresden china is made in Meissen; 2. Shooting stars are meteors; 3. Shortbread is a cake or cookie; 4. Jumping bean is a seed; 5. Lead pencil is of graphite; 6. Bald eagle is not bald; 7. Horned toads are lizards; 8. Firefly is a beetle; 9. Prairie dog is a rodent; 10. Catgut comes from sheep or horses.

A121 Letters Q5

If each letter is allocated its appropriate number in the alphabet – i.e., A=1, B=2 and so on – a magic square is formed whereby each horizontal, vertical and corner-to-corner line totals 34.

G	M	D	J
B	L	E	O
I	C	N	H
P	F	K	A